MW01244475

A Heavenly Christmas

A Heavenly Christmas

Enjoying the Presence of Jesus Everyday

A 31-Day Family Devotional

Craig Van Zandt

TATE PUBLISHING & Enterprises

A Heavenly Christmas
Copyright © 2010 by Craig Van Zandt. All rights reserved.

No part of this publication may be reproduced, stored in a retrieval system or transmitted in any way by any means, electronic, mechanical, photocopy, recording or otherwise without the prior permission of the author except as provided by USA copyright law.

Scripture quotations taken from the New American Standard Bible®, Copyright © 1960, 1962, 1963, 1968, 1971, 1972, 1973, 1975, 1977, 1995 by The Lockman Foundation. Used by permission.

The opinions expressed by the author are not necessarily those of Tate Publishing, LLC.

Published by Tate Publishing & Enterprises, LLC
127 E. Trade Center Terrace | Mustang, Oklahoma 73064 USA
1.888.361.9473 | www.tatepublishing.com

Tate Publishing is committed to excellence in the publishing industry. The company reflects the philosophy established by the founders, based on Psalm 68:11,
"The Lord gave the word and great was the company of those who published it."

Book design copyright © 2010 by Tate Publishing, LLC. All rights reserved.
Cover design by Chris Webb
Interior design by Joey Garrett

Published in the United States of America

ISBN: 978-1-61663-663-0
1. Religion/Christian Life / Devotional
2. Religion / Christian Life / Spiritual Growth
10.07.16

For today in the city of David there has been born for you a Savior; who is Jesus Christ the Lord.

Luke 2:11

Table of Contents

Section One: the Christmas Story and You

Section Two: Christmas and the "Presence" of Jesus

Section Three: Enjoying Christmas everyday!

Foreword

Being in pastoral ministry for twenty-plus years, I am always on the lookout for a book, devotional, article, or story that truly moves my heart from contemplation to transformation. I'm delighted to say that *A Heavenly Christmas: Enjoying the Presence of Jesus...Every Day* has done just that! It is insightful, inspiring, challenging, deep, practical, moving, and meaningful. I found myself in these pages, identifying with my own struggles of self-centeredness and doubt, longing for a life with Christ without restraints. Although the subtitle is, *A Thirty-one Day Family Devotion on Christmas,* Craig Van Zandt exhorts us to live our lives the way God intended...day by day, moment by moment, experiencing Christmas—the gift of God's Son in every fiber of our being. Thank you, Craig, for this precious book. I trust that you (the reader) will discover Jesus Christ in refreshing, life-changing and sustaining ways.

—Pastor Pat Gordan,
Bethel Baptist Church, Santa Rosa

Preface

There can be no greater experience in life than communion with our God. There can be no greater knowledge we can acquire in life than knowing him. There can be no greater purpose in life than to grow in the knowledge of our Savior and to experience his life to the full. In this devotional on "Christmas," I hope these things can be brought to life and be ever-increasing in our body, soul, and spirit.

These words in this devotion I have written in prayerful communion with the Lord. I have written them first for myself letting the Holy Spirit do his work in my life as he desires. In this regard these words are intimate and private. And though I am certainly not ashamed to share them, I am somewhat reluctant to think someone else would really want to read them. Second, I prayed the Lord would use these words as I shared them with my family—my wife and daughter. Any expectation beyond this rests in the heart and will of God for my life and this book.

There was initially no intent on writing a book. Through encouragement from my family and a few close friends, I trust the Lord to accomplish his will in and through my life. If he so desires to use these words, then let us enjoy the ride together as he so faithfully and intentionally moves in and through our lives in mysterious and certainly unexpected ways. Whether we eat or drink, work or sleep, whether we write or read, whatever we do, let us do it all and only for the glory of our gracious and most holy and compassionate Savior, the author of the true heavenly Christmas.

This book is divided into three sections. In the first section of our devotion, we will take a simple look at the Christmas story (Luke 2) and how it can affect and change us. In the second section of the devotion we will go into a little more depth of thought as we look at just twelve specific gifts the Lord has blessed us with by the "presence" of his life in us. In the third section of our look into Christmas, our focus will be on four ways in which we can keep his "presence" alive and growing in our day to day walk. Each day will consist of some scripture, reflective thoughts, prayer and some words I think the Lord would say to me. I enjoy imagining the Lord right here by my side, sharing Christmas, and sharing words of encouragement and exhortation. These words are certainly not Scripture nor meant to replace Scripture, though I hope they are all scriptural. They are just words that I use for myself to help make Jesus more personal in my life.

I can hardly express the depth of feeling of reverence and the humble privilege it is to commune with our God. It is with the greatest of care and responsibility as well as joyful freedom in the Lord that I write and share these words. It is my hope that God would use these words and ideas to first glorify himself, and second to bless us and move us to a perhaps a deeper experience and meaning to the living truth of Christmas. May God take these words that I have written, written in the weakness of my flesh and longing in my soul and spirit, and make good my mistakes and erroneous thinking. May you, dear reader, always check everything you hear and read against the veracity and inerrancy of Scripture.

Thank you for letting me part of your Christmas this year. May God the Father be praised for the unity of the Spirit in the body of Christ. Merry Christmas dear family, and may we see each new day as a Christmas day giving praise and glory to God in the name of Jesus.

Introduction

And the angel said to them, "Do not be afraid; for behold, I bring you good news of a great joy which shall be for all the people; for today in the city of David there has been born for you a Savior, who is Christ the Lord."

Luke 2:10–11

"Isn't there anybody who knows what Christmas is all about?"

This question comes from the mouth of babes, an animated babe anyway. Charlie Brown, in an exasperated tone and cry of frustration asks this question to whoever would listen, hoping someone had an answer. Linus takes his thumb out of his mouth and says, "I know what Christmas is all about, Charlie Brown." He then proceeds to the microphone, requests the lights be turned down, and then recites the Christmas story from the Gospel of Luke, chapter 2, "And in the same region there were some shepherds... glory to God in the highest, and on earth peace among men with whom he is pleased."

This is one of my favorite Christmas memories. Even now, at the age of fifty-five, I recall the scene as if it were yesterday. Linus, in his innocent and childlike voice, completes his recital and says, "This is what Christmas is all about, Charlie Brown", for today in the city of David, there has been born for you a Savior, who is Christ the Lord.

I did not understand the answer to Charlie Brown's question during the years of my youth, at least the way I needed to understand the answer, but it did stir in me something that told me Christmas is not about what I thought it was about; that is, presents and more presents, Christmas trees and decorations, relatives, and vacation from school. Though I did not know the Lord then, maybe it was stories and memories like this embedded in my family's Christmas traditions that kept me close to the truth of Christmas and out of trouble in my youthful years. It was not until in my young adult life that I truly did understand what the meaning of Christmas was and is all about. Actually, I am still growing in the knowledge and wisdom of what Christmas is about, as this is a lifelong adventure—growing in and *enjoying the presence of Jesus every day.* (2 Peter 1:1–2).

How would you answer this Charlie Brown question? The answers we get today on the streets of our culture range from the sad to the silly to the sublime.

"Christmas? It is just another manufactured holiday created by the retail industry to steal away our money ('to pick a man's pocket' as Ebenezer Scrooge would say), to make them rich(er). It's a sham, made up by manmade religion to keep people living in some kind of spiritual pipe dream, if not a guilt-ridden legalistic lifestyle of rules that only strangle one's human rights to make their own destiny. 'They' are forcing me to believe in what they believe in. I want no part of it! Bah! Humbug!"

"Yeah, Christmas, a time for parties and food and drink and reveling in a good time."

"Christmas is a time for children, you know, Santa and reindeer and presents and that kind of thing. It's a fun holiday to think about being a kid again."

"It is a time to celebrate life and nature and the oneness of the universal consciousness and the spirit of life in every living thing around us."

"I used to love Christmas, now I hate it. It only shows me how lonely and alone I am and all the things I once had but have no more."

"Christmas is about family and friends, sharing laughter, hopes, and dreams. It is about reconciling relationships and carrying on with rich family traditions."

"It is a time when we think more kindly and benevolent toward others less fortunate. A time to give and not be so selfish. A time for personal reflection."

"Oh yeah, Christmas, it is a time to go to church, to sing songs, to give and receive gifts, to celebrate life."

And, "Christmas is a time to celebrate and worship the life of Jesus, our Savior."

It is safe to say that we as a culture have lost the true meaning of Christmas. We have become sorely distracted by mankind's window dressing of twinkling lights, brightly colored ornaments, wintery scenes of Santa, his reindeer, the present-laden Christmas tree, and "holiday cheer," all of which lasts as long as a thin layer of ice on a sea of hot eggnog. Now please do not misunderstand me. I truly enjoy the festivities of a rich Christmas season and traditions, but I believe we have lost our way to the selfless heart of the Savior and found our way to the self-centered heart of man. We have turned from the celebration of the true life and *presence of Jesus,* to the fanciful life and *presents of Santa.* We have turned from the *worship and reverence of God in the flesh—Jesus,* to the *worship of self and the material world.*

We need more than Rudolph's shining red nose to find our way out of the dark clouds and stormy winds and rain of greed and humanistic priorities and thinking. We need the truth and *presence of Jesus,* the true light and life of mankind to save the heart and meaning of Christmas.

If there is any one thing our culture, our individual lives, and the church on the corner really need today, it is to find our way back to the true meaning of Christmas—the birth and life of the Savior.

"The hopes and fears through all the years, are met in Thee tonight," is the phrase in one of our favorite Christmas songs.

Hopes and *fears;* isn't this the way we live today? We hope beyond hope for "things" to work out, but we are not really sure what these "things" are and what the source of our hope is to begin with. And are there not so many fears that loom large in the landscape of our lives that consume us and control us and only feed our sense of helplessness and hopelessness? Understanding the true meaning of Christmas is a wonderful remedy for getting out from under the misaligned hopes and emotional fears and circumstances that seem to control us today.

Christmas really is for children; children of the Lord. There is childlikeness in all our hearts today. Though it may be *hidden* for safekeeping, *buried* for protection, or *wearing a disguise* to keep one's true need from the public (or family's) eye, it is there all the same. Jesus calls us to be childlike, not childish, but childlike in trust and faith in him. Needless to say, we have grown to be callous, cynical, skeptical, self-protective, and close-minded in our culture where man sits on the throne. Our hopes set on our fellow man have failed us and disappointed us. Thus, because of our hope in man and our fear of man, our childlike need and love for the truth of what Christmas is all about has been squelched. Our fears of our fellow man have overwhelmed us and control us. But should we plant our hopes in the Christmas truth of his life and give him our fears and worries, we will not be disappointed, for he will not fail us. This is his Christmas promise to us (Matthew 11:28; John 10:10, 14:27; Philippians 4:6–7; 1 Peter 2:6).

Christmas, the celebration and life of our Savior, is the answer to our blind hope and our paralyzing fears. In his life in us we have gifts of his character, his very *presence* enabling us to live a life above our fears to a life of freedom and true hope and security in him. Jesus has given to us beyond what we can really imagine. His *presence* in us cannot be exhausted, in that we have in him heavenly riches that will continue to pour forth into our souls each and every day. In these heavenly riches of h*is presence* in our lives, we have all we need to live abundantly in and above this earthly flesh where false hopes and emotional fears abound.

Christmas is not just a day or a season or a time of the year, even though as the song goes, "It's the most wonderful time of the year." Christmas is "more of Christ" (Christ/mas—more of) in our lives daily. As we choose to live in the "Christmas" truth, as we allow Christ Jesus to live more fully in our lives, his unconditional and selfless love, strength, wisdom, and power—*his presence* of life will flood us and flow through us in blessing him in blessing others all for the glory and exaltation of his holy name and life.

Let us get back to the heart of Christmas, the heart of the life and *presence of Jesus* our Savior, so we can once again (perhaps like our animated friends Charlie Brown and Linus) get back to the truth of a *heavenly Christmas* our gracious Savior would have for us.

I hope you enjoy the journey through these next few days. Remember, these truths are not just for the Christmas season, but for every day of our lives, for it is every day we can experience a *heavenly Christmas and enjoy the presence of Jesus.* "This is the day which the Lord has made; let us rejoice and be glad in it" (Psalm 118:24). This is the day to celebrate Christmas—the coming of our Lord Jesus to earth to don the flesh to save you and me. Let us celebrate with all our hearts and minds and with all our strength until he will soon come again to bring us home to his heart forever.

"This is what Christmas is all about, Charlie Brown, for today in the city of David there has been born for you a Savior, who is Christ the Lord." Amen? Amen and amen!

Section One

the Christmas Story and You

A Look at Luke 2:1–20

Now it came about in those days that a decree went out from Caesar Augustus, that a census be taken of all the inhabited earth...And all were proceeding to register for the census, everyone to his own city. And Joseph also went up from Galilee, from the city of Nazareth, to Judea, to the city of David, which is called Bethlehem because he was of the house and family of David, in order to register along with Mary who was engaged to him, and was with child. And it came about that while they were there, the days were completed for her to give birth. And she gave birth to her firstborn Son; and she wrapped him in cloths, and laid him in a manger, because there was no room for them in the inn.

And in the same region there were some shepherds staying out in the fields, and keeping watch over their flock by night. And an angel of the Lord suddenly stood before them, and the glory of the Lord shone around them; and they were terribly frightened. And the angel said to them, 'Do not be afraid; for behold, I bring you good news of a great joy which shall be for all the people; for today in the city of David there has been born for you a Savior, who is Christ the Lord. And this will be a sign for you; you will find a baby wrapped in cloths, and lying in a manger.' And suddenly there appeared with the angel a multitude of the heavenly host praising God, and saying, 'Glory to God in the highest, and on earth peace among men whom he is pleased.'

And it came about when the angels had gone away from them into heaven, that the shepherds began saying to one another, 'Let us go straight to Bethlehem then, and see this thing that has happened which the Lord has made known to us.'

And they came in haste and found their way to Mary and Joseph and the baby as he lay in the manger. And when they had seen this, they told them about this Child. And all who heard it wondered at the things which were told them by the shepherds. But Mary treasured up all these things, pondering them in her heart. And the shepherds went back, glorifying and praising God for all that they had heard and seen, just as had been told them.

Day One

the Unopened Gift

☙

It is Christmastime. The anticipation, especially from the children, has been building for many days, if not weeks. And you will have to admit, the child in you wishes for such Christmas joy and expectation, especially now in this time of your life, this time amid the hectic schedule and pressures of living and the covered up, perhaps disguised, emotions and disquieted rumblings in your soul that render you a bit too somber, cynical, and joyless.

There is a crispness to the winter's air that breathes of freshness and purity as frost lays heavy on the ground in the early morning stillness. The decorations have been set out in a dazzling display of lights and tinseling glitter. Figurines of angels, Santa, reindeer, Mary and Joseph, the Babe, wise men, camels, and a host of farm animals adorn front lawns, mantels, and shelves throughout the yard and house. Cookies and goodies have been baked by the hundreds, and candy canes, peppermint bark, and many shapes and sizes of chocolate are found everywhere.

There is joy and unusual feelings of selflessness and giving that invade your being, even through the toughness and struggle of life that has calloused on your heart and soul. Though there are times of stress of shopping and the busyness of going here and there, it is a happy time of year. There is much reminiscing and conversing of old times, memories of lost loved ones that bring forth both tears and smiles, as well as many hopes and dreams shared about tomorrow. Families coming together perhaps for the only time of the year find lots of laughter and even tears as lives are being shared.

It is Christmas morning. The stockings that were once empty and hanging over the fireplace are now stuffed with goodies ready to be dumped (ever so carefully of course) on the floor to be enjoyed. Presents, adorned with bright Christmas wrapping paper and ribbon, are still at this point neatly gathered under the tree. And the tree, standing with *tinsel tinseling* and lights illuminating, carefully if not meticulously decorated for this time of the year, is just waiting to be plundered of the treasures under its branches.

The house feels warm to the body, soul and the spirit as the fire in the hearth glows with enrapturing light and inviting heat while the aroma of hot chocolate and apple cider permeates the air with a winter's scent of the joy of Christmas morning. You feel warm and content, yet with an edge of anticipation of the traditional celebration of laughter and family fellowship at the passing out and opening of the gifts.

This year there is a very special gift under the tree. It is something you made just for that very special someone. It was made out of love and sacrifice and you cannot wait for this special someone to receive and open your gift. You know it is the perfect gift and can bring great joy and satisfaction. You care far more in giving this one gift than receiving a thousand gifts yourself.

All are gathered around the tree with fun anticipation of seeing their gifts received, and of course, receiving gifts from loved ones as well. Slowly it starts as each gift is opened and appreciated. Soon the pace quickens as more gifts are passed. It is a happy time, and any thought of the "real world" is left out of the magic of this Christmas morning.

Finally your gift is handed to that special someone. Your

anticipation and excitement is at its peak; you cannot wait to share this gift with the one you love so dearly.

What happens next, you will never forget. While all the other gifts given and shared by everybody to everybody, the times of laughter and the catching up on the lives of your family will have been forgotten, this one moment will not be forgotten, at least for you. Your gift is opened; that special, unique, personalized and most precious gift you could ever give, and then is almost without recognition covered back up and carelessly tossed in the pile with the other gifts. In fact as you see it, it lands almost out of the way from the others.

You are devastated. You can't believe it. This gift of love, all of the effort, the thought that has gone into making it, so much joyful anticipation as you longingly waited to give your gift away; all have been so carelessly cast aside. How could anybody be so unappreciative? How could anyone be so insensitive and cold?

ଅ

Now, let us make this personal; think about how you would feel if you had planned to give a most precious gift of love and sacrifice only to have it cast aside. And, could you be that person to whom the gift was given and with hardly a second thought simply cast it aside, perhaps never to be opened or thought of again?

Well, with this Christmas season upon us, I dare say we are guilty of doing this far more often than we care to admit. And this is not just on Christmas morning, and not just concerning a physical present given to us by a loved one. This attitude and unappreciative reaction is part of us nearly every morning of every day. When we react like this, we sorely disappoint the Giver in a callous manner when every morning we wake up to a new Christmas day—a new Christ-made day and shun his gift of life. It is the Lord's heartfelt and personal gift of life and opportunity given to us that we reject and cast aside for the sad purpose of the lust and arrogance of living for our own day.

Please do not shy away from the truth of this reality or be

afraid of the depth of the emotional hurt this causes our Lord. For it is true, every day, every morning, the Lord has given to you with his life—His presence, his perfect gift for you to enjoy and to find perfect peace and purpose and spiritual and emotional prosperity and abundance.

Think again on how you would feel when a gift you so affectionately crafted was rejected by someone you love. Consider the depth of hurtful emotions that would encompass you. The Lord feels this hurt and sadness far more than we could really imagine. It is not just one day a year he might feel such emotion, it is everyday we wake up and choose to ignore or even throw away his gift of life for the day, that he feels such grief. Just as a father or mother desiring the best for their children feels almost unbearable pain when their child rebels and rejects their love or is hurt or tragically hurts themselves, so the Lord, our heavenly Parent, feels hurt to a much greater degree when we reject him.

I wonder if we can truly fathom Christmas the way it is meant to be. Not so much the decorations, presents, and "holiday cheer," which are really not important at all, but in reverence and awe and joy of receiving and sharing the gift of Christ every day. I wonder can we truly hear the wonder and beauty of a *heavenly Christmas* in our busy lives so full of … self?

ɞ

"Dear Father, we need Christmas. We need the miracle of Christmas, the truth of Christmas, the wonder of Christmas, and we need the reason and life of Christmas. We need Jesus. Guide us this day, this month, throughout all the years and help us make everyday a Christmas day, a day in which we give our lives in daily surrender to you and receive from you the purpose and power of your presence. Teach us daily what Christmas is really all about. This is something we constantly need to be reminded about. May our hearts be open and may you be pleased to teach us and guide us into your presence. In Jesus name, Amen.

Day Two

Christmas Did Not Just Happen

&

C hristmas: what a wonderful time of the year. And if we would take just a little more time than we usually do we would discover that Christmas is a mysterious and wondrous time of the year. It is a time when the Infinite Creator with purity of heart compassionately touches the finite, needful, empty, and fallen heart of man; when the wondrous light of illuminating truth and life overshadows the darkness of lust, want, envy, doubt, despair, and death; when the true hope of eternal peace and life becomes an inner joy of security and knowledge, replacing a false sense of happiness and independence that deceptively leads to frustration, desperation and despair. And it is a time when God so ordained that history should kiss the future in the present of today, making this day, this Christ-given day, a truly wondrous time of celebration and experience of the Creator moving in the hearts of created man—of you and me!

Let us quiet our hearts and lives and be still to hear and experience the wonder of this *Heavenly Christmas*. Let us give way to the promptings of the Holy Spirit and cast aside our worries, our fears, our hectic and self-centered agendas and lives, our prideful arrogance in what we think we know and what we think we need, and open our hearts to the moving truth and life of the Holy Spirit of this Christmas season. Let us close our eyes to the glaring lights and distracting decorations that physically illuminate this time of the year and open our spiritual eyes to the truth and splendor, the incredible color and majesty and wonder of a *Heavenly Christmas.*

It is truly a wondrous and mysterious time when the sovereign plan of God so profoundly incorporates the will of man as he orchestrates his will and purpose in history in the story–His story of Christmas.

ॐ

"Oh Lord, let us learn from this Christmas story about the wonderful and wondrous truths concerning our own lives in your heart. There is so much we do not know about you. There is so much we misunderstand about the true celebration of what Christmas is all about. There is so much we need to know as we humbly request that you would enlighten and enliven our hearts and minds to hear your glorious truth in celebration of this wondrous *Heavenly Christmas* in this wonderful Christmas season."

ॐ

It came about in those days …

Luke 2:1

Christmas did not just happen. This is not a day of chance or any arbitrary day! "But when the fullness of the time came, God sent forth his Son, born of a woman, born under the Law" (Galatians 4:4). This time, this day in history is the day God had in his sovereignty established to put on the flesh and begin a final work in completing the plan of redemption for his children—for you and for me.

A truly mysterious and wondrous part of Christmas is

that God uses the choices of man to make his eternal plan of redemption come about. We cannot understand how this works, but it does (Isaiah 55:8–9; Psalm 103:19). Man makes "free will" choices for his life, yet God directs his steps so that things work out for his pleasure and purpose (Proverbs 16:9; Philippians 2:13; Romans 8:28). Man and his freedom to choose are integral pieces of the formula for the unfolding of history (HIS STORY) of God's will and purpose.

It is this appointed time that one of the final pieces of the puzzle of God's redemption of man comes together. (Galatians 4:4; Isaiah 7:14). The pieces of the puzzle put together to arrive at this ordained first Christmas morn are numerous and transcend many years and centuries, and they are far out of reach of man's manipulation and planning and even comprehension.

There is an Old Testament prophecy that states the Messiah would be "cut off" (Daniel 9:25–26/Nehemiah 2:1–8; Isaiah 53:8). That is, he would be killed by way of crucifixion (Psalm 22:14–18) on a certain day! That means his day of birth must have come at just the right time for his days to be completed. It also means that Rome, the empire in which crucifixion began, would have to be in power (it wasn't at the time of this prophecy, nor was crucifixion a way of execution). And that Rome would have established such a means of transportation and news communication to the world that the news of the gospel could be spread at this specific and appointed time. This means that the people of Israel and the dynamics within the Jewish people and their relationship with the Roman Empire would be in such a state that all that transpired concerning Jesus would be providentially worked out through the choices of man though mysteriously purposed and orchestrated by God throughout history at that particular time (Micah 5:2; Daniel 9:25; Isaiah 7:14; Matthew 2:6–18).

Think of the spread of the gospel through Paul and Peter and the rest of the apostles. God knew whom he was going to use and when he was going to use them. Their birth and life histories were by no accident or by chance! Nor are your birth and life history and future controlled by accident or chance (Psalm 139; Philippians 1:6; Psalm 138:8). We all have freedom to make our choices, but God's will shall be done. This we cannot fully understand.

God's providential hand in history (his story) means that at just the right time, Joseph, who had to come from Bethlehem but live in Nazareth, would meet and become engaged to Mary. At just the right time, Mary, who would live in Nazareth, would be visited by the Holy Spirit to give her the greatest gift for mankind—Jesus. A main player in this real life play of Christmas was Caesar Augustus, who at just the right time issued a decree for a census to be taken, so that at just the right time, Joseph and Mary would have to return to Bethlehem (the place where it was prophesied that the Messiah would be born (Micah 5:2), yet come from Nazareth of Galilee. It was just at the right time for this to happen as Mary was near the number of days of her pregnancy that they entered to the town where there would be no room for them. All this and so many more details had to happen at just the right time and just the right order for Jesus to enter this life, live his life, minister his Word, and then be crucified (*would be cut off*) on this prophesied day in a prophesied way (Daniel 9:25–26; Nehemiah 2:1–8)! There are so many details (prophetic history) that had to fall into place over centuries of time and hundreds of miles of geography and through many apparent personal choices of the main players in this Christmas story since the beginning of time that at just the right time all this took place in the right order! Chance had absolutely nothing to do with the wonder of the Christmas miracle.

As it is with his story of Christmas, so it is with his story with you and me. Chance, coincidence, and luck are not part of our life's formula. Though we may not be able to see all the pieces of the puzzle of our life: past, future, and even those before us in the present, God's hand is putting his story, his picture of your life together at this very moment. What a wonder he is. And what a wonder you are, and this not from our perspective, but from his (Genesis 1:27; Psalm 37:23; 139:1–6; 14–16; Ephesians 2:10)!

೮ು

"My Sovereign King, my Lord, just as you have so mysteriously and intricately put together the events of history, you so care the same about the unfolding of my steps in my life today. I am so blinded by my own plans for tomorrow and my mistakes of yesterday that I just cannot see your working and orchestration of my life today. There seem to be so many scattered pieces of the puzzle of my life I just cannot figure out where they all go. I give these pieces over to you and I thank you for knowing how everything fits together. What a wonder it is that you would have such intimate care and make such an intimate involvement in my life. Where I was yesterday, what I am doing today, where I am going tomorrow have all worked out and will be worked out in your timing—what a wondrous truth this is! Lord, I pray this Christmas season that I would perhaps for the first time open your gift of life and purpose for me and truly follow your ways and your plans and your will for me. Thank you, my sovereign Lord, for your never-ending thoughts, gifts, and plans you have for me . . . "

೮ು

My Christmas wonder, I am pleased to be with you today. I am pleased to have thought of you, created you, and to instill in you and work through you for my good will and pleasure (Phil. 1:6, 2:13). Nothing about you is by chance. Though you may look at where you are right now, and think what bad or good luck controls your life, there is really no chance or luck involved in my plan for you. As I related to my people Israel that I know the plans I have for them, plans for welfare and not for calamity to give them a future and a hope (Jer. 29:11), so it is with you too. To see from this truth and perspective I need you to walk by faith and no longer by what you can understand and see with your physical senses (Heb. 11). My ways and thoughts are far above yours (Isa. 55:8–9). Now, right here, is perfect for you and me to grow closer together. May you enjoy this day I have made for you, for this purpose (Ps. 118:24, 139:16).

Day Three

You Did Not Just Happen

∞

And Joseph also went up from…

Luke 2:4

It is not by chance that you are where you are. There is no happenstance or luck or coincidence about God or about his ways for your life. He, in his unexplainable and unfathomable omniscience (all-knowing) and sovereign providence and orchestration of life leaves nothing to chance or "fate" concerning his precious child—you. Sure you may have made decisions to get you where you are physically, emotionally and even spiritually, which may not be in his "perfect will," but it is the Lord motivated by his love that uses your decisions to bring you to this spiritual point in your life (Proverbs 16:9; 20:24), even to when and where you are reading this!

As Scripture says, "My frame was not hidden from Thee, when I was made in secret, and skillfully wrought in the depths of the earth. Thine eyes have seen my unformed substance; and in Thy book they were all written, the days that were ordained for me, when as yet there was not one of them" (Psalm 139: 15–16). The

Word of the Holy Spirit testifies a most wonderful and comforting bit of truth for our lives: "I will instruct you and teach you in the way you should go; I will counsel you with my eye upon you" (Psalm 32:8). "He will guide you on paths of righteousness" (Psalm 23:3). "It is God who began a good work in you and he is faithful to complete it" (Philippians 1:6; 1 Thessalonians 5:24). It should be a wonder to us that the almighty God who holds all things together, who stretches out the heavens, who made and placed and named all the stars (Psalm 147:4), knows your name, knows your fears, doubts, dreams, anxieties, knows your needs and prayers, even before you do (Isaiah 65:24; Matt. 6:8)! And he not only knows all these things, he lovingly and compassionately cares for them (1 Peter 5:7; Matt. 6:33; Ps. 18:19, 86:13)!

We do not know much about Joseph, but what we do know is inspiring. He was probably a hard-working and honest man that had a big problem. He was betrothed to a pregnant woman. Today, sadly, this may seem normal and accepted, but then it was quite an unacceptable scenario. Do you think he had questions and doubts about Mary? Yes, big time. Do you think he was emotionally hurt and unsure? I would think he had to have been. Did he have questions about what to do? How could he not? Was his honor and reputation at stake here? Absolutely. Being a righteous man he was ready to "put her away secretly" (Matthew 1:19). But what did he do? Well, after getting a heavenly visitor, he surrendered his will, put aside his own way of perceiving the situation, put away his own plans for his life, and trusted the Lord! Talk about faith!

Joseph was just a man, a very humble and contrite man used of the Lord. And, what about Mary? A young woman, most likely excited about her betrothal and the plans of a wedding and new life with her future husband; excited about having children and the precious treasures of raising a family of her own; she couldn't wait! And then a visitor came from above to change whatever plans she may have had, at least for the time being. "A child in me, what will everybody think? What will Joseph do? Will I be cast out, shunned, stoned to death?" Before these thoughts got too far in her mind, Mary simply said with contrition of heart and a soulful selfless attitude and desire to please the Lord, "Behold, the bondslave of the Lord; be it done to me according to your word" (Luke 1:38).

Wow, talk about faith! Where would you be if you found yourself in their shoes, (or sandals or bare-feet as the case may be)? So willing? So agreeable? So calm? So alive with a contrite and selfless and faithfully willing heart?

Maybe you do not know where or why or who you really are today. Maybe you are not sure of your purpose or what the will of God is for your life. Maybe you are thinking "How could God use a person like me? I have failed miserably. I have no confidence in my flesh (which is actually a good thing). I have messed up my responsibilities." Kind of sounds like Moses, does it not? And what did God do with Moses? Think of Jacob, a conniving fellow really, or Jonah, who ran away from the Lord's call, or even David, a murder and adulterer? What of Zaccheus or Matthew, rich and successful men by way of, shall we say, very unethical and immoral means, were touched by the Lord to become new people? Or how about Mary Magdalene or the Samaritan woman at the well, or the sinful woman who wept at the Lord's feet? They were all blessed and used of the Lord for his glory. Your purpose, like that of Joseph or Mary or Abraham or David or a host of others, is to not worry about where you have been, what you have done, or what you do not know, especially about your own life, but to know the life of the Savior and surrender your all for his all.

So you too, like these biblical individuals, with such diverse personalities, hang-ups, strengths and weaknesses, challenges, doubts and fears, can be used of the Lord, right where you are, even under unimaginable circumstances! For both Mary and Joseph, whose lives were not turning out the way they had planned, with a contrite and willing heart thought less of themselves and more of the grace and will and power of God in their lives. They trusted God more than they trusted themselves. They trusted God when the world around them did not really have a clue as to what was going on. And the world in which they lived, I am almost sure, let them know about it in no less then condemning words and tones.

I cannot exactly tell you how you hear God's call on your life. I wish at times it would be clearer—like an angel in a dream or a vision or a voice (as scary as that may be). I do know that, in the communion of holy and humble prayer, He reveals himself to us in ways too deep for words and even rational understanding (Rom. 8:26; Phil. 4:6–7). Through our humble lifestyle of surrendered prayer His abiding and consuming presence will flood us with His peace and joy and strength overwhelming and taking away our worries and fears and out-of-control feelings and emotions (John 16:33; 1John 4:18). Though you may not be sure where you are heading, surrender that worry to him and trust him to show you his way (Proverbs 3:5–6). His peace will be your constant companion. His peace will assure you of his presence (John 14:27, 16:33; Ps. 23). *The Lord is the portion of my inheritance and my cup, says the psalmist, … because he is at my right hand, I will not be shaken. Therefore my heart is glad, and my glory rejoices … Thou wilt make know to me the path of life; in Thy presence is fullness of joy; in Thy right hand there are pleasures forever* (Ps. 16:5, 9–10).

ॐ

"Lord, can you really use me today? Like Joseph and Mary, I long to hear your calling, your purpose for my life. Help me hear this today Lord. Open my ears to hear the miracle and wonder of Christmas. Help me forget about my own way of thinking and planning, help me get out of my own way, and your way, to solely look unto you for your plan and direction for your life in me. You are the Author and Perfector of my life and faith (Heb. 12:2). *Whom have I in heaven but Thee? And besides Thee, I desire nothing on earth. My flesh and my heart may fail, but God is the strength of my heart and my portion forever* (Ps. 73:25–26). Thank you for leading me and guarding me, even though I may not be sure where it is you are leading. I will follow the beautiful music of your Christmas call…"

℣

My child, rest in me this Christmas season and everyday of the year. I know you do not think highly of yourself. Though it may sound strange, but in thinking this, you actually are thinking too highly of yourself. You think about you too much. In either case, false humility or pride, you have put yourself in the center of your life. I have created you so that only I should be in the center of your life. You want to find your purpose in life, you want to know my will, you want to live to please me, these are good things but you must do something first. You must first come to me for the sake of me (Matt. 11:28; Ps. 46:10). As you do this, rest in the truth that you are my purposeful Christmas child and right where you are is where you can best serve me, worship me and be with me. You did not just happen to be born in the world without me knowing about it, without me giving you life. You are not a mistake; I have purposed you in my heart from eternity past. Today is the greatest day of your life because it is here that I can and will work through you. It is this day that our love can and will grow. It is this day, right where you are, that together we can take a step toward my plan for you. Rejoice in this day as if it is Christmas day and receive the gift of contentment and purposeful security as you surrender your all to my will so that I might be my all in you.

Day Four

Worry, at Christmas?

છ

… And she gave birth to her first-born Son; and she wrapped him in cloths, and laid him in a manger, because there was no room for them in the inn.

Luke 2:7

I wonder if there was not just a little bit of panic from Joseph and Mary when they could not find a sensible room to rest, have shelter, and, have a baby! I wonder if Joseph went from door to door frantically asking for a place to stay, a place for help as Mary quite well could have been in labor with the Child. I wonder what doubts or questions Joseph and Mary were prayerfully asking of God during this time: "Father, please guide us to a room … ," "Lord, what are you doing? Why did you lead us here only to not find a room for the birth of our baby?" "What about the baby, Lord? What about the baby?" "C'mon, Lord, we are following your ways. What are you waiting for?"

I wonder how many times in our lives we live by little faith and big frantic prayers. If you are like me, I know it is far too often we have to admit this to ourselves. But just like with Joseph and Mary, quite possibly frantic in prayer for their need, God was with them. Of course he was with them, this was his event, his doing; he was responsible; he was in control, wasn't he?

This is where God really shines—in seemingly impossible and desperate situations. Abraham was desperate when he held that knife above Isaac's chest. Moses and company were desperate when their feet were getting wet by the Red Sea and Egypt's military were bearing down on them leaving no way of escape. Elijah was desperate running away from Jezebel who wanted to kill him. Paul was desperate in fear of his life many times, under persecution from the Jews and the Romans that did not want to hear what he had to say. Jesus was desperate as he prayed to the Father that "this cup" should pass from him, sweating drops like blood as he was praying.

The good news is that in our desperation, God is not in desperation. He is forever calmer and forever in control. Isn't this a wonderful thing? He is not controlled by his emotions as we are. He does not capriciously or arbitrarily deal with us based on whether we do what is right or wrong. He will convict us, discipline us and encourage us perfectly! He is never shocked, therefore never emotionally rocked over anything that happens in our life. God is an emotional God, and whether he acts in love or anger, jealousy (his definition of jealousy, not ours—big difference here) or grace, holiness or mercy, he always acts in his perfect and holy and goodness of character (Psalm 145:9; 100:5; 31:19). Though we may seldom see our life's situations in such calmness and control, let us be assured God is working out his purpose for us. If we are in his hands, then we are in the safest place possible, even amidst the storms in life, just like Joseph and Mary were, even though there was *no room for them*.

Did they need to be frantic, if indeed they were? No. Do we need to be frantic in our lives as we feel a need from within screaming out at us to find protection, provision, or satisfaction? No. God is with us. This is just what the Christmas story is all about—Immanuel, God with us, now and forevermore (Isaiah 7:14; Matthew 28:20). Let us be encouraged that just as God answered their prayers in just the right time—his time, he too will answer your prayers in his time, in his way, which by the way is the best way. Be prepared though, his way and answers for your life just may be quite different than anything you might expect— The King of kings, Lord of lords, the Creator of the universe, born in a stable, amid straw and dirt and animals? Who would have thought that (Isaiah 55:8–9)?

So, when perchance you feel that there may be no room for you in this world, when you feel out of place, when you are not accepted, when you are condescendingly dismissed, fret not; put your faith in the One who is the sovereign over all. If God is for you, who can be against you (Psalm 56, 73:25)?

બ્ઝ

"Dear Savior, thank you for your faithfulness. Thank you for hearing my prayers even though I may not hear your answer. It is only that I am not listening properly that I do not hear or see an answer. I am listening for what I want to hear, not necessarily what you want to tell me. I am blinded by the franticness of my circumstances and out-of-control emotions that seem so overwhelming and hopeless. Thank you for this glorious Christmas celebration–this very Christ created day (Ps. 118:24) and this gift of your providential love and grace working out in my life. Help me overcome my limited perspective and petty need for answers or signs from you in my way, in my time, for my satisfaction. I look to you, but, Lord, I must confess I look to you to answer my needs, my prayers, in my way. It is often I look beyond you to what you can do for me. You know all I need, even before I do, how amazing is that (Isaiah 65:24; Psalm 139:4; Mtt. 6:8)? You know what is best for me. Help me Lord, look beyond my want to seeing you only—my only true want and need (Ps. 73:25; 145:14–16). You are the answer yourself! You do answer my prayers all the time. Help me see this. I prayerfully rest in your sovereign control over all life and over my life. How can I be so anxious even in my prayer life when the truth is you are God over all and have my best in the center of your heart and thoughts and plans (Ps. 16:5–6). Lord, you have already made things work out for my life. Guide me to follow your will and desire for me. Thank you, my loving Savior, for this assurance and for loving me this way."

෨

Merry Christmas, my chosen one. You seem to worry over many things. You seem to worry over the things you think you need to do in this world. You worry over accumulating possessions or status or a particular self-image, and then when you have them you worry over maintaining them, holding on to them and not losing them. You worry over pleasing me and knowing exactly what my will is for you. All this worry is tying you in knots, it is making you apprehensive, it is stealing the joy and the freedom I desire for you, it is robbing us of our intimate relationship. Remember my friends Mary and Martha? Martha was worried over much, even about serving me. This worry kept her from what was really important, just being with me (Luke 19:38–42). Mary chose the 'good part", she sat down and simply took in my presence. This is what I want you do to.

Though you may panic when your life and the life around you seems to be whirling out of control, please know that I am in complete control. You panic because you do not feel in control. When this happens your life is flooded with anxiety and fear. This fear robs you of my calming presence. My disciples were in a boat in a storm. They panicked with fear because they took their eyes off of me and put them on themselves. I guess they did not see me in the boat with them, calmly sleeping. They did not see me because they did not yet know me as they should. *Do you not care that we are perishing,* they asked (Mk. 4:38). They had not yet learned that I was their life and that with me regardless of the storm around them I would see them through. Take this Christmas time and wrap your worries in a box and give them to me. Cast them from the storm-tossed-boat that is your life. In return I will give you my calming peace (John 14:27, 16:33; Phil. 4:6–7). Be still and fret not any longer for I am with you, always!

Day Five

There's Lots of Room ... in the Manger

‰

… No room for him …

Luke 2:7

Of course the people in this sleepy and out of the way town had no idea of who just entered their little community. I am sure those behind the closed doors who did not help did not know it was the most important Mom and Dad, the most important baby, and the most important delivery in the history of mankind! Those who closed their doors did so perhaps out of fear; they closed or did not open their doors not wanting to get involved, or for a simple reason of not wanting to be inconvenienced.

There was no room for them in the inn. Could it be the truth that no one wanted to make room for them? How is it with you? Would you have let them (him) in? Would you have made time and room to help? We know the history. Whether one is a Christian or not, we can so easily and casually read the historical account that there was no room for them, but we should not let the fact that this is history detract from the necessity of answering these needed questions for the heart today: What keeps the Savior out of the "inn" of our hearts and lives? What keeps Jesus from being in *full* control of our lives today?

Is it because we are afraid? Are we afraid of what others will think; afraid of the unknown or afraid of putting our life's destiny into the hands of a God we cannot physically see or hear clearly? Maybe we are afraid of what we think would be the sacrifices and or changes we might have to make in our lives to follow Jesus. We fear a radical change and we do not want to make a radical change, thus, we do nothing. We think we are comfortable where we are and we do not want anything to "rock the boat", as it were.

For many of us (if not all of us) it could be a "pride thing" that we make no room for the Lord of Christmas in our hearts. In our pride we hold on to who we think we are, what we have made for ourselves and the status, power and control we have over our own lives and the lives of others. We are 'god of our own destiny', right? At one time or another we all could easily play the part of the *rich young ruler* who asked Jesus about eternal life. He heard an answer he did not want to hear: *go and sell all you own, give to the poor, and then come and follow me.* It was his riches on earth he was clinging to for identity and purpose that kept him from the eternal blessing and riches of the Lord (Matt. 19:16–26). We may not have earthly riches like this rich young ruler, but we cherish and cling to if not idolize the riches of our own "self-life" where we sit on the throne as king!

Our reluctance and stubbornness to let Jesus into the control room of our lives maybe because of simple inconvenience. Another time we will think about it, another time when we have time, when it does not get in the way with what we *think* we *really* have to do, when it does not get in the way of our personal agenda and aspirations. Accepting this Christmas truth might require a change in our priorities, our core beliefs and our value system–the way we do things in business, relationships or social life–our culturally learned lifestyle. It is the busyness and *obsession* with our "self-life" that keeps the Lord's very important business–the will, purpose and power of his life out of our life.

The wonderful news to all of us who have closed our hearts to the gift and life of the Savior is that each day, each morning can be like a Christmas morning (Lamentations 3:22). It can be a morning when the Lord will faithfully knock on your heart's door to see that if today, perhaps, you will invite him into your life and decision-making process. He is knocking on your heart's door to see if you will come out and follow him today—on this Christ-given day he has planned for you. The good news is that the gift of this baby is the answer to all fear and turmoil, dreams and ambitions, to insecurity and unstable identity, to all questions and doubts. We will never be able to walk freely in life with his blessing until we let him in to the "inn" of our hearts to live and make himself at home. Is he at home in your heart, or are you making him feel like a visiting guest, an unwanted guest, or even a stranger? "Blessed are the pure in heart for they shall see God", says our Lord (Matt. 5:8). Is your heart singularly focused and devoted to him, is it pure this way, not distracted by the allurements of the world? This is the only way that we can experience (see) God in our lives to the full. The good and wondrous news is that he is excited to come into our hearts and lives, to lead us to his banquet table of his life and purpose, now and eternally.

ॐ

"My merciful wonderful counselor and healer, my Lord and Savior, forgive me for only making room in my heart for myself. My life is so cluttered with worry and fear that I feel I am trapped in a dark closet of self. I confess it is difficult for me to let you in to my heart completely because it is so full of myself and so full of garbage that would not please you. The truth is there is part of me that still wants to be in charge and in control of my life. I fear not being in control of what may or may not happen to me. I have set up my own idol of myself and want to cherish it, protect it, and worship it. I have made my life my own 'holy of holies,' and allow only myself to enter in. This idolatrous worship has only gotten me from one frying pan into another. Help me, Lord, and forgive me, Lord, for worshiping my own sense and need of comfort, acceptance, position, and possession in life. Lord, only you are worthy to be worshiped. Help me cast away all that keeps my heart full of this worldly life, so that you may enter in and have full control, just as you will. Thank you, Lord, for never giving up on me, for always being there with me, for promising your eternal provision of all I need and all I could ever truly desire. May my heart be a comfortable home for you."

ॐ

My dear hard-hearted child, do you know that I thoroughly enjoy spending time with you? I am praying that your heart be softened today. My desire is to live fully through you today as never before (John 10:10; Eph. 3:19). Know that I will not push my way into your life. I will stand at your heart's door and knock (Rev. 3:20). I will wait to be invited in. What makes it difficult for you to invite me in to reign is a prideful stance and the infiltration of the riches and priorities of the world you have let into your life (1John 2:15–17; Ps. 66:18; Isa. 59:2). These things have kept me off the throne of your life. Trust not in either yourself or these earthly riches and wisdom for they will fail you. Please know that I will not fail you.

It is in your heart where I wish to reign, and it is in my heart where I wish you to reside (John 15:1- 8). As it is, in the weakness of the flesh, I only reside in your heart and not reign, and you try to reign over me. Thus, your life is defined by great discontent, division and anxiety. Fear not to let me into your life, completely and without condition. You think you will have to give up some of what you so treasure in the world if you let me in. This is quite true; you will have to give up that which you hold on to in this world. But realize what you are holding on to, even your self-identity, is only a substitute, a falsely satisfying fleshy fix that leaves you empty and wanting more and more (John 3:27; Phil. 3:19; 2Cor. 6:12). Be assured I will give you more than you can imagine in the presence of my peace and joy and purpose and love (Matt. 19:29; John 10:10; Ps. 16:11, 36:7–9). Trust my heart and my love for you (Prov. 3:5–6). Fear no more, strive no more for your life of self. Know that my love that surpasses knowledge will fill you up to all the fullness of God who is able to do exceedingly abundantly beyond all that you ask or think according to his great power (Eph. 3:19–20).

Day Six

With What Do You Clothe Jesus?

&

...Wrapped in cloths and laid him in a manger...

Luke 2:7

Mary and Joseph did the best they could with what they had for their baby. If they could have done more or better, they would have. What matters is that they gave him their all and did their best. By the way, have you ever thought of this simple fact that the greatest king, the wisest man, the most honest and noble and righteous ruler, the most influential leader, the greatest orator, the best friend, the most compassionate healer and the most selfless lover of our souls that has ever lived was born in the dirt of a stable or in a cave? Talk about rising from humble beginnings. In fact, he spent his whole life in humble beginnings and surroundings. Not in a monk-like requirement of deprivation, but by joyful choice and godly priorities of not thinking more highly of himself. It wasn't a self-pity wallowing of "I am not good enough," "I don't deserve favor from anybody." It was an honest humility gained from knowing and resting in the true value of his life and identity in his

Father's heart and eyes. By the way, can you imagine that—Jesus not thinking more highly of himself? "Hey look guys, what are these, rags around me? Is that a donkey I hear over there? What is that smell? Peuuuweee! C'mon guys, I am King of kings and Lord of lords. Give me some respect!"

Was there fanfare for this king? No, but there were angels in heaven and stars from above shining down upon him. Were there royalty, princes, and kings there to honor his coming to earth? No, unless you would consider lowly "workin'-for-a-livin'" shepherds and a few farm animals chewing on straw in such light. Was this family of Joseph, Mary, and now baby Jesus given the keys to the city, gifts of diapers, baby blankets, baby clothes, strollers, rattles, tickets to Disneyland and the like? Nope. They barely had clothes enough to cover him.

Does this lead you to examine your own view of self, where you came from, and what you have and do not appreciate? Does this make you think about what is really important and of value in this life of plenty? Does this make you want to reevaluate your priorities in life that have been set by a world and culture principled by money, power, possessions, status, physical image, and position? The Spirit writes with great encouragement and conviction that *not even when one has an abundance does his life consist of his possessions* (Luke 12:15), and, *The Lord is the portion of my inheritance and my cup; Thou dost support my lot… indeed, my heritage is beautiful to me* (Ps. 16:5–6). How much more inner peace we would experience if we had this perspective of truth guiding our lives.

Jesus was given rags to wear—nothing royal, nothing special, nothing worthy of his true being. Jesus was given rags to wear in place of our rags that we deserve. He was given rags to wear so we might be given his robes of righteousness (2 Corinthians 5:21). Even in his infancy, and throughout his life, he took our dirt, the dirt of this world upon him, so we might be cleansed from such dirt—the dirt of sin and flesh.

Imagine you are a missionary or just visiting a mission field of one of the dirtiest places on earth. Children there have not taken a bath for … ever. They do not even know what a bath is like. The clothes they wear are caked with dirt, grime, waste, and who knows what else. On your visit there, a young child comes up to you and asks for your cool-looking shirt. He kind of tugs at his shirt with one hand while tugging on your shirt with the other letting you know he would like to exchange his for yours. You have at least a handful of shirts and to give this shirt would mean no sacrifice to you. The child on the other hand has no other, and this one is badly torn. What do you do?

Would you exchange shirts? I mean would you take your clean shirt off and put on his dirty shirt (yes, not just hold it at arm's length, but put it on with all its grime and stench!)? This is what Jesus did and does for us. We are that child, and he is that missionary.

I wonder, how long is it after we receive his wonderful sacrificial and selfless gift of his robe of righteousness, do we get it dirty in the world, do we neglect its care, do we care to not even put it on? Jesus wore our rags, willingly, joyfully, every day of his life. He did this until he was stripped of these dirty and blood-stained rags and was hung on a cross to take the naked dirt of our sin upon his body and put to death our sinful and dirty flesh and robes of self-righteousness! What a gift he has given us.

With what do we clothe Jesus as he lives in us? What attitude do we put on? What emotion and behavior do we choose to let define us as we walk among the saved and unsaved? What priority and what principles do we wear to 'make a living' in this life? What does the world see about us and in us in regard to a Christ-like witness? Do we wear him well? Do we wear him like an undergarment not to be seen, or do we not wear him at all?

How do we wear in honor his robes of righteousness he so graciously and selflessly gives us? Joseph and Mary did their best to care for Jesus. They gave up their own interests, their own lives for him. How do you do your best to care for Jesus? Give him the gift of love and care this Christmas season. Lay your own your self-interests at his feet and take up his interests before your own (Phil. 2:4). Give him your life with reckless abandon holding back nothing for yourself (Mk. 8:34–38). Give Him your best with all your body, soul and spirit, with all your strength (Matt. 22:37; Deut. 10:12)!

∞

"My precious Jesus, may I honor you by wearing your gift of your robe of righteousness to the best of my ability with all my heart, mind, soul, and in all my strength. And may I give you my best so that your best and your glory may shine through me in exalting your name (1Cor. 10:31). This Christmas Day, every day, my Lord, may my life be a gift back to you as you have first given life to me. Forgive me when I do not wear you well, when I wear the rags of my own pride and righteousness promoting self rather than exalting you. Forgive me, Lord, that I do not offer you my best, but offer you an effort that is secondary at best. Help me, Lord, cast aside all I put before you as rubbish (Philippians 3:8) that I might gain the blessing of your selfless life in me. Thank you, gracious Savior, for giving me your all. I pray with help from the Holy Spirit as I surrender my all to you that you would find my gift of my life acceptable and honorable. And may I wear your righteousness with utmost humility and honor. Thank you, Lord, for this privilege and honor."

∞

Merry Christmas, my child who seems to wander off so frequently; I wish to adorn you with my raiment of righteousness. Like the father of the prodigal who with a longing heart patiently waited for his child to return so he could give him the best he could offer, so I wait for you. I want to give you the best I can offer. I want to take your clothes of self-righteousness which are stained and soiled with the sweat of pride, and give you my radiant white robe of righteousness.

This is what I want for you. In this robe you will

never be found naked in vulnerability, ashamed in your dependence upon me, lost in the ways of the world or without all your needs being met. Though the world would throw mud on you and spit on you in their slander and persecution, these will not stick to or stain my robe on you. It is my truth that has cleansed you, both internally and externally (John 15:3, 17:16–19).

In return for my robe of righteousness I simply want your dirty rags with which you try to clothe yourself. It is your robe of self-righteousness, self-dependence, self-confidence, self-love, and self-worship that keeps you stained and defined by the world, and keeps you struggling in your physical, emotional and spiritual life for me. Give to me these rags and receive your new identity by wearing my righteousness. Live no longer with man-centered attitudes and principles and priorities of this world. Put me on and no longer make any provision for the lust of the flesh (Rom. 13:14; Ps. 37:1–11). My child, yes I want your rags, but more importantly I want to give you my righteousness. Let me do this for you this Christmas time and throughout your life.

Day Seven

Lost in Your Own Life

&

And in the same region there were some shepherds staying out in the fields, and keeping watch over their flock by night...

Luke 2:8

Wouldn't it be a wonder to be one of those shepherds that Christmas Eve night? Have you ever thought about why this majestic heavenly angel appeared to these lowly shepherds and not to the religious or political or social elite? They were bringing an announcement of the King of kings (1 Timothy 6:15), the Savior to mankind (1 John 4:14), the one whom the government will rest upon his shoulders (Isaiah 9:6), and the high priest forever (Hebrews 4:14)! You would think such an announcement would be for royalty and for those in authority wouldn't you?

These shepherds were perhaps representative of an everyday people in everyday life, living day to day, doing the same thing over and over again, like you and me and Joe and Jane Jones next door. Perhaps these shepherds carried on a continual conversation throughout the day and into the evening, mumbling and grumbling to one another about the *mundaneness* of the life they felt they were trapped in, or the miscarriage of justice they could do little to nothing about, or the unfairness in life that all seemed so overwhelming. These shepherds were living life, simply trying to satisfy and find fulfillment for their disquieted and discontent lives by the shallow and unfulfilling ways of the world around them. These shepherds were raising sheep to be mercilessly slaughtered on a sacrificial alter of their religious practices as a way of trying to please their holy God. Over and over again, lamb after lamb, one at a time, never-ending cycle of raising living animals to die—it seemed. "What's the use? What's the purpose? Isn't there a better way?" Little did they know that better way, the better life was right around the next bend, the next pasture, as it were. It is these shepherds that would be first to rejoice at the true sacrificial Lamb of God. They would be the first to understand their hard routine of life of working for religion and working at religion would be at an end (Mtt: 11:28–30). They would no longer have to work twenty-four hours a day providing for and protecting the sheep from the harm and dangers of this life, only to have them be killed on an altar of religion and life.

These shepherds could very well have been lost in their own lives, blinded by their limited vision and aimless search for identity. Just like you and me, the emotional noise of discontentment, the selfish want and soulful need for acceptance and purpose brought about a sense of hopelessness in the routine of life that arrested a true joy and peace of God. These shepherds, in whatever condition they were in, like us, need to experience this *heavenly Christmas*. We need the message of life and hope—the living Word and living sound of the wonder and miracle of Christmas. These shepherds, like us today, need to hear the good news, the wonder of this *heavenly Christmas* in the One who has come into this life—the Lamb of God - the True Shepherd who will guard us from evil. It is the True Shepherd who will take away all fear, who will provide meaningful purpose and work that is eternal, who will lift us out of the *mundaneness* of man's way of living and bring peace and joy and contentment to our disquieted and turbulent souls. These shepherds, like us, need to be shepherded by the one True Shepherd who will lead us to his green pastures, still waters, where there is an abundance of life and living (Psalm 23).

Do you feel stuck in a rut in life that only seems to get deeper and full of engulfing mud? Do you ever have the thought that "life" is just going on all around you and you are missing the point, the meaning, the joy, and the purpose? What is it you are shepherding in your heart? That is, what are you spending your life's energy on in caring for (Mtt. 6:19–21)? What are you so tenaciously and stubbornly guarding? Yourself? Some financial gain? Some forbidden pleasure? Some professional, social, personal advancement of your name (Luke 12:15)? Our True Shepherd calls out to us to leave the career of furthering our own agenda and living in the self-righteousness mode, to take up the call to pursue holiness and to pursue him just as he has made us to be in him (Philippians 3:12–14; 1Pet. 1:15). Our one True Shepherd calls out to us in his inviting voice:

> Ho! Everyone who thirsts, come to the waters; and you who have no money come, buy and eat. Come, buy wine and milk without money and without cost. Why do you spend money for what is not bread and your wages for what does not satisfy? Listen carefully to me, and eat what is good, and delight yourself in abundance. Incline your ear and come to me. Listen, that you may live ...
>
> Isaiah 55:1–3

And in Matthew:

> Come to me, all who are weary and heavy-laden, and I will give you rest. Take my yoke upon you, and learn from me, for

I am gentle and humble in heart; and you shall find rest for your souls. For my yoke is easy, and my load is light

Matthew 11:28–30

I cannot think of any more of a comforting invitation than this, "come". Come just as you are. Jesus would say to us, "If you are brokenhearted, come, and I will give you comfort and rest. If you are laden with guilt of sin and worry, doubt and fear, come, and I will give you peace. If you are lost in a sea of emotions that are tossing you to and fro, and imprisoning thoughts paralyzing your next step, come to me and I will give you freedom to rejoice once again and truly live in the joy of your salvation." Are you there, my friend? Thank the Lord he has come for you!

&

"Thank you, my God, for wanting more for me than I could ever want for myself. Thank you for making my life special, unique, not routine or mundane. Help me, Lord, see your purpose in me, in what I am doing and where I am. Lord, only you can make my life content, full, and abundant. Only you can make my life count. Thank you Lord, that you can and will use me wherever I am. Thank you for your faithfulness and patience in my life. May my life, Lord, be used for your glory and purpose. May I honor you in all I do, think, and say. May you smile today because of your child—this child, me."

&

My precious lost one, lost in this world of so many enticements and distractions, lost in self of so many temptations and lusts, find your way to me today. I am your shepherd and I call you to my pasture of my life (Ps. 23). I call you to want for only me and no longer for the feeding of your flesh. I call you to partake of my eternal spring of quiet water that will restore your weary soul (Ps. 23:2; John 4:14). I call you to my paths of righteousness on which your feet will not stumble, where I will lead you by holding your hand (Ps. 23:3; 18:35–36; Isa. 41:13). I call you to confidence in my presence as I walk with you through the midst of the storms of this life (Ps. 23:4, 27:1–5; Heb. 4:16). I call you to my standards of life and truth and to my discipline and counsel that will produce fruit of love and godly righteousness (Ps. 23:4, 32:8; Heb. 12:10–11). I call you to claim victory in battle over the flesh and this world (Ps. 23:5; Rom. 8:37; 2Cor. 2:14; 1John 5:4). I call you to have a very merry Christmas in living with me all the days of your life.

Day Eight

Not a Piece of Fruitcake, the Peace of God!

&

And an angel of the Lord suddenly stood before them, and the glory of the Lord shone around them; and they were terribly frightened…

Luke 2:9

These shepherds certainly were frightened by this heavenly angelic visitor and experience, but do you think their fear went to a deeper level of their being—deeper than just a physical reflex or reaction of fear? It would not be unreasonable to think this fear went straight to and opened up their needy and hurting heart in a most humbling experience of their lives.

If we honestly think about it, do we not let a lot of our daily decisions and thinking and actions be dictated and controlled by some sort of fear? Most of the time we might attempt to mask these fears with a busyness in life, a self-imposed importance and confidence of self (identity) and the influence and control we have in the world of family, friends, and business. Sometimes we will hide our fears in the achievement of performance or the attainment of things that we can call our own. "This is what I

did; this is what I have. What a full life I have made for myself!"
All the while deep down, we know there is something missing.

Control is a huge issue for us all. Our fears, whether we are
aware of them or not, are directly related and proportional to
how much we try to control our lives and how much we let life
and circumstances around us control us. The more we fear the
more we try to control, and the more we try to control, the more
we enhance the fear of losing control and being controlled, which
our prideful heart does not like. Our prideful and stubborn bent
for independence puts up a very tough exterior (façade) that
we hide behind, keeping our fears hidden, not wanting to show
weakness or vulnerability. There is great fear in the thought of
not being loved or accepted, or of not being of purpose and significance. We might often fear being alone, of being rejected or
of being ridiculed. We fear failing and even trying because of
the fear of failing. In any case we hide or disguise our fear with a
façade of being in control and having our "act together."

The shepherd's fear, like ours, may stem from the knowledge
of their sinful state of being—the things they do, think, and say,
their unkind if not malicious motivations to get ahead, their greed
and lust for pleasure or earthly treasure or to gain more prestige
or power or a higher position. I wonder if they instantly became
acutely aware of their attitude of greed, lust, and ungratefulness.
Maybe this angel appeared right in the middle of a 'gripe session'
these shepherds were enjoying? Could that happen to you and
me? I will answer "yes" for me.

And now they see a heavenly vision, so pure, so righteous, so
holy in contrast to the darkness of their own heart and lives. Was
it going to be judgment time for them? They most likely knew
the scriptural stories of angels that came to minister judgment
to the unbelieving Jews and Gentiles in the world. For whatever reason, physically, spiritually, and emotionally, they were
wrapped in and controlled by fear.

Our list of potential and real fears can go on and on. In any
case, it is because of fear and insecurity that we try to control
our lives and the lives around us. These shepherds, like us, were

definitely not in control of this situation, they did not know what was going to happen. In seeing this radiant heavenly vision of an angel, they must have felt vulnerable, weak, desperate, and helpless. These shepherds needed a way out of their fears. These shepherds needed peace—a godly peace—they needed their God, their creator, and this they would soon realize, and, see. They did not know their fears and uncertainties in life could only be met in the love of whom the angels came to announce!

The Holy Word tells us many times over to "fear not." If you are in a place right now and fear of the unknown has gripped you, know this first and foremost: your God, our Lord Jesus, is bigger than any fear you have and is bigger than anything that produces such fear. Take comfort in his glorious infiniteness and sovereignty and know he has hold of you, even though you might feel or think you do not have hold of him. Remember these words of truth and comfort as a gift from him to you this Christmas season: Do not fear, for I am with you; do not anxiously look about you, for I am your God. I will strengthen you, surely I will help you, surely I will uphold you with My righteous right hand ... for I am the Lord your God, who upholds your right hand ... (Isa. 41:10–13).

&

"Dear Mighty Father, there is great fear in my life, I must admit. It is this way because of all the things I try to control but cannot control. It is hard for me to let go of all that life is, all that I want and think I need and think is important. Help me, Lord, to fear you, be in awe of you, be in continual wonder of you, instead of fearing man and the things that I might gain or lose in this world. Help me, Lord, to hold on to nothing, save you. Your perfect love for me casts out all fear this life brings to my heart. Help me know this love, Lord, that I can let go of my needs and desires for my life—a need to be selfishly loved. Help me see that as I grab onto your selfless and sacrificial and perfect love, I have everything I could ever need in you. In your perfect love I live in your presence without fear of man or the world or even of my own flesh. In your love there is great freedom from fear and a great freedom and assurance of faith that you are all in all (2Cor. 3:17; 1John 4:18). Thank you for being my refuge and safe harbor and perfect provider (Ps. 31:3, 46:1–3, 62:1–2, 73:26). Because of you I truly have no need to fear."

ဢ

Indeed my fearful one, I am the answer to your fear (1John 4:18). As you grow in the knowledge of me, you grow in my love and security, thus, your growth in love and security in your life. You fear because you are insecure. You are insecure because you try to control, but you cannot control, even your life. You try to control because of your prideful heart that has walked away from dependence upon me to be dependent upon only yourself. This is a sure recipe for fear. I have come to show you who I am. I am your Savior, your Creator, your only true source of life and light, of peace and joy, and truth and security. Let me ask you a question, why do you fear and worry if you know I am all-powerful and that I love you completely? You fear because you still believe more in yourself than you do in me. My prayer for you this Christmas season, this very day is to 'fear not'. You can do this, you can 'fear not', if your surrender your life to me, completely and without restraint. You can do this if you give me control of your life and strive no longer to control, either yourself, others, circumstances and especially me. I came to dispel your fears and to replace your fears with my love and the truth and security of my faithfulness. Give yourself a gift this day and receive my gift of security and peace and love. Throw your fear and anxiety and insecurity at my feet and pick up my peace. Rest assured, I will deal with your fears once and for all. I am the only one who can.

Day Nine

Something Infinitely Better

&

And the angel said to them: "Do not be afraid, for behold I bring you good news of great joy which shall be for all the people…

Luke 2:10

Have you ever wondered what the Lord himself or this angel perhaps would say to you should he appear right where you are today? Would the words be words of warning, condemnation, or commendation? Would they be gentle, firm, or harsh? Whatever words they might be, I do know they would be perfect for the moment—just what we need (not necessarily want) to hear. Now, put yourself in the shepherd's position—frightened in a jumbled, mixed-up, emotional world of want and need and fear. The angel's words to you are, "Do not be afraid." Do not fear any longer about your position in life, your emotional longing or pain, your spiritual doubts and questions, your life's circumstances that so control your soulful and spiritual health. Do not worry or fear over the guilt of your mistakes and your sin that have for so long kept you imprisoned.

Do not fear, but know one has come to take away your sin and your fear and to give you life and assurance, peace and freedom.

"Fear not," for there is news of "great joy!" Boy, do we need to take these words to heart today! "Fear not, there is great joy, great peace, great security, great assurance that everything will be all right." This promise is for a joy beyond our comprehension, but not beyond our apprehension (Phil. 4:7 & John 14:27). A joy and peace we can have but not fully understand, an answer to the routine and even the despair in life. It is a joy beyond and outside of us, beyond our fleshly reach; thus, it does not depend upon our own strength or wisdom to attain. This is really good news and crucially important to understand. There is nothing we can do in this life to find this peace and joy our soul so longs for. This is a good thing because if we could find such peace and joy, it would only last as long as our circumstances or strength and faith in self would hold out. This certainly would not be for a very long time. It would be rather short and frustratingly intermittent at best. It would be susceptible to being stolen away or lost. The wonderfully good news of this joy and peace of heavenly origin, given to us from the one above through the one who came as a babe—Jesus, our Lord, is eternal! It is rooted in his faithfulness which will never falter, not ours which will always falter. It is a joy and peace with heavenly power and duration, with a heavenly purpose, made just for you!

What would be the greatest bit of news you could receive today? To have someone say, "I love you" for the first time, for the ten-thousandth time, or after a major relational hurt or blowout? To hear you have been hired for a job? To hear your lost loved one has returned home? Your mortgage and all your debts have been paid off? To hear you have inherited a million dollars, or that you have received an "A" on your exam, or a promotion at work? As wonderfully good news as all this is, there is something infinitely better. It is from the Lord. "Today, my child, I am going to walk with you. I love you. Fear not, for I will never leave you. I will lead you in my path of righteousness." Do you know we get this Christmas gift every day? Can you hear this wonder of Christmas truth, *Fear not, I am with you, always* (Matt. 28:20)?

These shepherds needed something new in their life. They were tired, weary and worn down and heavy laden with fears and anxieties they perhaps were not even aware of. How goes it with you? What good news awaited them and awaits you!

ɞ

"Thank you, Lord, for hearing my prayers. Thank you, Lord, for being my living hope and my living joy and peace and my living answer to my need. Thank you, Lord, that your news of great joy is eternal and new for me each day. Help me wake up each day as a Christmas Day and hear your words, "Fear not my child, I have taken care of life today. Come along with me, and together we will experience great things of great joy. Even through the times that might not be much fun, with me, together, we can rejoice in each others company." Thank you, Lord, as I prayerfully walk through my day with you, or I should say, as I walk with you through your day, I will be refreshed and led by your Spirit. I shall choose not to fear because in your love there is perfect peace that surpasses understanding (1 John 4:18; Philippians 4:7), because your loving kindness is better than life (Psalm 63:3, 84:10). What a great truth and reality this is to live in. Thank you, dearest Father, that my day is new and planted in you."

ɞ

My child, do you believe these words of my Spirit, 'Thy loving kindness is better than life?' This is news of great joy! In this world you grope around as in the dark hoping to find your answers to life. This is a problem. It is a problem because you are asking yourself (and me) the wrong questions. 'What is my purpose in life?', and "who am I?", are good questions, but in the flesh you can spend all your life's energy in pursuit of these questions and still not find the answer that will satisfy your soul. 'Who is God?' is the right question. Until you are asking this question and looking to me for the answer, any other searching will be as if you are just groping in the dark. Come to me for the sake of me and I will give you all that you need to know–I will fill you with myself (Matt. 6:33; John 14:27). You seem to continually be looking for greener pastures. Well, I am your greener pastures; I am your greenest pasture you can ever find. The good news of great joy is my promise to you of a new way, a new life - an eternal life. It is a way out of the routine of this world, and into a vibrant, exciting and blissful relationship with me. In this truth as you let me flood you with this relational experience you will see that my lovingkindness is better than life. You will never find more life, more energy, more purpose, move love and acceptance than in me and spending time with me. Be pleased to grow in the knowledge of me as I am pleased for you to do so.

Day Ten

Savior for Me, Really?

&

For today in the city of David there has been born for you a
Savior, who is Christ the Lord …

Luke 2:11

If you want the answer to your life, here it is, "… born *for
you* a Savior." Do you hear that, "for you"! Our sovereign
and mighty, our compassionate and loving heavenly Father
had this day—this Christmas Day of celebration—this visitation
of the Infinite heavenly to the finite earth planned before time,
matter, and space began! The magnitude of this truth—his sovereign plan for redeeming man coupled with the incomprehensible truth that Jesus, God the Son, came down from heaven and
put on the "flesh and bones" of this babe in the manger—should
be an awesome wonder for us all. This day was foretold by the
prophets, and this truth is treasured and lived out by millions
today, as has been throughout history and will be into tomorrow.

Do you want to know something that will bless your Christmas
stockings right off the mantel? If you read Paul's letter to the
Ephesians, chapter 2 verses 8–10, you will see that you are God's

workmanship—his skillful and attentive and passionate work of poetry. And he has created you for good works, which he prepared beforehand! He had thoughts and a plan and a love for you before your parents did, before the foundations of this earth (Psalm 139:16)! You, little 'ole unworthy, useless you! Yes, you are his loved one, and he has a purpose for you!

If you haven't gotten this impact yet, let's make this intimately personal. Jesus has been born for *you!* Don't let this Christmas story, this Christmas truth, pass you by. This Christmas gift of the Father—our Savior Jesus Christ—is for you! What is Christmas all about? It is about one thing and one thing only ultimately. It is about you and the Lord and the relationship he would have with you now and eternally. His gift to you, his desire for you, his love for you, his hope for you, his life for you is ever-present and eternal!

A Savior implies that we need to be saved from something. What is it you have been saved from? Why do we today need a Savior? He came to save you from your sins and eternal separation from the Holy Father. He came to give you the most precious and valuable gift ever given to mankind. His gift was life in and of himself.

We need a Savior because we have been born into sinful flesh and have a sinful nature (Rom. 3:23; Ps. 51:5). We need to be saved from this sinful life that repels the life and truth of God (Rom. 1:18–25; 1Cor. 1:21–23, 2:14; John 3:16). If left to ourselves, like a dog returning to the mess he made, we too without God would return to the mess of our flesh time after time (Proverbs 26:11). But God in his mercy does not want us to linger in the non-life, this deadness of flesh and spirit (Romans 6:1–13—count how many times there is a reference to death). Therefore, before the foundations, he knew what would happen with men and made a way of our salvation. Through the life of Jesus, through his death and resurrection, we are saved. What a gift (John 5:24; Romans 6:23; 1Cor. 15:3–4; 1John 2:2; Ephesians 2:8–9)!

And we are saved from the penalty of sin—death, and the power of sin and death. Sin no longer has its claws tenaciously and *mercilessly* dug into us. Death no longer has its sting (1 Corinthians 15:54–57). It no longer holds sway over our fear-laden emotions. In Jesus we now have the power to not sin and to not fear (John 8:11). We have the power to step out of the prison of our flesh and sin and be free to live a new life in him and for him (Romans 6) as he lives in us. We are saved from our selves (Galatians 2:20). Unfortunately, though our flesh is dead, we resurrect it to life in our lusts and pride and independence, doing the bidding of our enemy—the devil and our flesh (James 1:13). On our own we are our own worst and greatest enemy. The good news of truth is that we no longer need to live on our own, or live as a pawn to the spiritual enemy (1 John 4:4). That is why the Lord tells us to deny self, take up the cross—that instrument of death—and follow him (Mark 8:34). Of course God knows we cannot save ourselves; we need a Savior (see epilogue). We need a supernatural plan that comes from outside this world, outside ourselves, a plan of heavenly origin and heavenly power! What a wise God we have. What a loving God we have. What a great God we have!

There are times I just feel completely useless and purposeless! Do you ever feel this way? This is a lie from the pit of darkness and the *father of lies,* the devil. This lie comes alive in us as we move away from his truth and listen to our feelings and the world around us saying we are not good enough, pretty enough, rich enough, smart enough, or many other *enoughs.* Though the world may not think you are worthy, though you may not think yourself worthy, do you know what is truly amazing? Jesus thinks you are worthy. You are worthy enough for him to leave his glorious throne in heaven, put on the decaying life of flesh of his creation, and die a humiliating death at the hands of his own creation, whom he loved. This is how worthy you are. He is your Savior, yours, yours, yours!

I am sure the shepherds, upon hearing such news, were amazed and perhaps also wondering if these things could be true. Are you there with the shepherds, asking the same thing? What greater news, what greater peace and joy could there be?

&

"Lord, your grace is amazing, your love unfathomable, your mercy without bounds. Thank you, Lord, for in all you do, it is good. Thank you, Lord, for dying for me. Thank you, Lord, for living for me. Thank you, Lord, for praying for me. Thank you, Lord, for being for me. What greater assurance in life can I have but this? There is none. Thank you that in your name, in your life, because of who you are, you saved me out of this darkness and control of sin and death. You came this Christmas morning to save me from myself and to save me for you! In your name there is my assurance of life, peace, and provision, for all I need now and forevermore."

&

I know your name my dear one. I have offered life to you and you have received life from me. My gift of life to you is very personal. You did not receive the gift of eternal life because perhaps your mother or father knew me, not because your pastor or best friend or relative had eternal life, or because you did something to earn it. I offered my gift to you with no connections to anyone or anything else. It is between me and you. It was my pleasure to do so (Ps. 18:19, 115:3; Heb. 12:2). Though you may feel estranged in your relationships, where you might feel an emptiness and a lack of secure trust, know that I am for you, personally. I know when you rise up and sit down, I understand all that is in your heart; I am wherever you are; I have woven you together in your mother's womb; I have made you fearfully and wonderfully; I have written the number of days I have ordained for you; I think about you constantly–you could not number my thoughts about you (Ps. 139). I am with you always and nothing will ever separate you from me (Rom. 8:38–; John 10:28). When you are weary and afraid I will strengthen you (Isa. 40:29, 41:10); when you stumble I will hold you up (Ps. 56:13); I will counsel and guide you with my eye on you (Ps. 32:8); and, I will fill your cup to overflowing (Ps. 23:5). I am for you, will you be for me?

Day Eleven

Oh Look, a Sign. Turn in Here

&

And this will be a sign for you; you will find a baby wrapped in clothes, and lying in a manger…

Luke 2:12

Do you ever think to yourself, "If only I truly knew God was real in my life. If only I could get a sign, some tangible evidence to believe he is real and he is who he says he is and, he truly cares about me. If I only truly knew what I am supposed to do with my life; what is the purpose to my life; just what am I dong here?"

Have you ever asked God for some sort of sign, if not for clear direction, to just let you know that he is here and that he cares? What kind of sign would you even ask for: an answered prayer?, money from heaven?, an immediate change of circumstances? Like our brother Thomas (I will let you call him "doubting" if you wish), would we only be satisfied or happy if we could see and feel his scars or hear is voice audibly? What sign would prove to you that God really does care and it is really God doing the answering? Would you need a parting of the Red Sea type experience, or something that any Hollywood special effects expert would be in awe of? Or would you be satisfied with something a little smaller, like reading his Word and experiencing peace? (O, dare we give ourselves the opportunity or the time for such needful and simple things (2Cor. 11:3).

I have gotten many signs that God is real and that he cares, though none as big as the parting of the Red Sea. You probably have too if you think about it. In fact, just as I was typing this today, I was prayerfully thinking about a bit of a strain in my relationship with my daughter, asking the Lord to help. At that moment, the phone rang, and guess who it was? My daughter, calling me to tell me she just arrived at school safely (she is a new driver so she needs to check in with us) and that she is sorry for the distance in our relationship! Wow! This is not a coincidence; it did not just happen to happen. It was a "God thing," shall we say.

The question is, what do we do with these signs? Do we cherish and remember them so that in some future time of trauma or testing we would not have to respond and react in panic, anxiety, fear, or hopelessness, but in calmness knowing that God is a faithful and good God? Do I let his signs change my perspective and outlook and attitude on life? Israel repeatedly forgot their God (Psalm 106), and we know what their history is like. Do we want to live like this as well?

As much as we might want such a direct intervention from God (and what a blessing it is when we get an answer so obvious), whether we get an answer—a sign or not—we must know that we already have a sign, an eternal sign that will never change or fade away. We must go back to the baby in the manger—Jesus! Numerous prophecies have been fulfilled in his birth, life, death, and resurrection; the testimonies of his life from day one throughout history; the impact of his life and truth are innumerable. Please do not overlook this very important point: this sign is not just on Christmas Day on which we should meditate, it is a sign of a heavenly Christmas to ponder every day—to experience his presence every day!

The prophecies came true. This real flesh and blood life, this real-life ministry, this real birth, life, death, and resurrection are our sign of his love for us. Jesus is the only sign we need. He is our only life we need. Remember this is personal. This will be a sign *for you!*

Do not be blinded by your wayward emotions run amuck or the emotion and struggle of the times, which is so easy to do. When in your darkness of trouble, doubt, fear, or suffering, realize his heavenly beacon of light and life is forever shining directly to you. I know it may be hard to see, but if we could remember the reality of his life and his personal love for you, this will bring a peaceful light to your at times oppressive darkness, if we let it.

I wonder if the shepherds were beginning to see out of their own darkness this sign of truth, light and life? In this silent and holy night of Christmas, can you hear the chorus of heaven made just for you?

Where are you right now? Are you roaming around in the darkness of your own night of doubt, insecurity, or unstable hope? You most likely are not shepherding sheep for your purpose in life, but you are doing something that defines your purpose and identity. The angel came to these shepherds, these "working for a living" people to tell them of a new way, a new meaning, a new purpose and wisdom and strength for life—a new life in the Savior. The shepherds needed to follow the sign—the Light, to see their salvation and their purpose. Let us, too, follow their lead.

&

"Dear blessed one, my friend and Savior, I pray not to see with my eyes or to necessarily have to understand it all with my mind, there is no way I could. But I would ask you to enlighten my heart to experience your truth in a way that is new for me. All along in life I have rested upon my strength, mind and senses to figure things out. I no longer want to rest and live in myself and live in my own way. But by faith, as a child, I pray to rest securely in you.

These shepherds, like me, may have been looking for and waiting for some sign from you to feel secure in their life. So unexpected and so wonderful in your infinite wisdom you gave them and us this sign that would be for all time. May I always see this sign of your love and sacrifice for me as I so desire to honor this gift every day with my life. Thank you for this gift–this eternal sign of this baby born in this world that I might be born in you."

ೞ

Merry Christmas, my child. Close your eyes of want and of pride and seek me first (Mtt. 6:33). Do not look for something in this world to satisfy your hunger of the flesh. In your weakness of flesh you seek for answers, even a sign from me. In doing so, you often overlook me. Just think of one answered prayer. That was all about me, not about you. Do you know why you do not see more answered prayer? It is because you are looking for *your* answer, not mine. I answer prayers all the time, you just miss them because you are looking for another answer. If you want assurance of my life committed to you, of my love faithful and fervent for you, of my presence always with you, just remember the Christmas story. Meditate on the wonder and mystery of it all. Take to heart the sacrifice I made for you and with this, the promise to you that I will come again to receive you to myself (John 14:1–3). Be patient my Christmas child and open your eyes to the splendor and majesty of creation around you, including your very body and life (Ps. 139). Let this assure you of who I am and my love for you. Nothing or no one could ever have made the universe and all it contains except me (Isa. 42:5–6, 45:18). My Christmas gift to you is everyday in the splendor and awesome wonder of the creation all around you; it is my love and life for you.

Day Twelve

Do You Get It? Do You Hear the Wonder of This Heavenly Christmas?

୧୦

And suddenly there appeared with the angel a multitude of the heavenly host praising God and singing, "Glory to God in the highest, and on earth peace among men with whom he is pleased. And it came about when the angels had gone away from them into heaven, that the shepherds began saying to one another, 'let us go straight to Bethlehem then, and see this thing that has happened that the Lord has made known to us. And they came in haste and found their way to Mary and Joseph, and the baby as he lay in the manger. And when they had seen this, they made known the statement which had been told them about this Child. And all who heard it wondered at the things which were told them by the shepherds. But Mary treasured up all these things, pondering them in her heart. And the shepherds went back, glorifying and praising God for all that they heard and seen just as had been told them.

Luke 2:13–20

Mary treasured up all the wonderful things spoken to her about her son. We can make Mary's prayer of praise ours: "My soul exalts the Lord, and my spirit has rejoiced in God my Savior. For he has regard for the humble state of his bondslave; for behold, from this time on all generations will count me blessed. For the Mighty one has done great things for me; and holy is his name. And his mercy is upon generation after generation toward those who fear him" (Luke 1:46–50).

Do you know the Lord has great regard and has great love for you? You should.

Do you know you are blessed of the Lord on High? You should.

Do you believe the Mighty One has done great things for you? You should.

Do you know his mercy, grace, love, and thoughts are showering down upon you daily? You should.

Why should you believe these things? You should believe them because they are true. And because they are true, let us exalt the Lord in our hearts and let our soul and spirit and body rejoice in the freedom and truth of God our Savior in our lives.

This Christmas Day, which is every day, let the solemnity and the heavenly joy that filled Mary's heart, fill your heart. Exalt and rejoice in the Lord. Bow down in peaceful, soul-satisfying, and uplifting humility, and surrender as his bondslave. He has blessed you with his promises for your life and his presence in your life. He has done and will continue to do great and wondrous things for you. His mercy and love's perfect desire is for you!

Now, concerning what we let into our hearts, the question for the day is this: In this day in which we hear and see so many evil and perverse attitudes and actions in life, as well as so many sorrowful and hurtful things surrounding us, all demanding our attention, what do you let into your heart? What do you ponder throughout the day? What is it that you let control your thinking? There can be no more important questions than these. For what you let enter your heart and mind to ruminate on will determine what you will show in attitude, emotion, and behavior (Matthew 12:34–35; 15:16–20; Proverbs 23:7).

Do you think of Jesus and his life, his will, his peace, his desire, his love, his holiness, his sacrifice, his purpose, his gift of life to you and in you? Do you think on what is true, honorable, lovely, right, pure, etc. (Philippians 4:8)? Do you let the peace of Christ and the word of Christ richly dwell and rule in your hearts (Col. 3:15–16)? Or are your thoughts consumed with what pleasures and riches and glory you can get from the world or what you have to do in the world to get ahead and how to be a success? Are you focused on how you look, what you have or do not have, what others say about you, etc., etc., etc.? What are the images, words, thoughts, and emotions you dwell on? Are they wholesome, peaceful, comforting, or do they promote lust, discontent, irritability, even violence? Just think of all the violence and sexual immorality and permissiveness in popular night-time TV entertainment, including professional sports that we let enter in our hearts without a second thought. And if you are so brave to let the Spirit do the diagnosing, what have you unwittingly allowed yourself to become callous to? What moral and ethical compromises have you made for the sake of being entertained and of pleasing self?

Mary did not have to look far for what life was about. She saw her life in her arms.

Mary did not have all the answers. She did not know all the doctrines. She made mistakes just like you and me. Beyond all that could be distracting to her real life, she knew the answer to life was in her arms. She knew what her life was all about. She knew the source of peace and contentment was in her arms and in her heart. This is what she meditatively pondered upon with gratefulness and awe. Are you with Mary, or is your heart, elsewhere?

Mary did not receive any Christmas gift other than her child— the Savior—yet she celebrated the first Christmas in pure joy and humility, servanthood, and appreciation for this Christmas gift. What will you do with your gift of the Savior? Will you rejoice in his presence and gift of life, or shun his gift and focus on the gifts you have made for yourself apart from him (John 15:5)?

The sound and experience of Christmas can only be heard from your heart—the place where God has made for only himself to dwell. Left to ourselves the sound of Christmas, of life, is this: it is the disquieted and noisy heart and lives of a wayward self, lost in the purposeless routine of self-centered living without a vital relationship with the Babe of Christmas. It is the blaring scream of discontent and anxiety amidst the busyness of the day and the fleshly and sensual priorities and fearful emotions of a sinful life and an elusive and unsatisfied hope.

Looking upon the Savior, the sound of Christmas is this: it is this discordant sound of our flesh drowned out by the awesome stillness and majesty and soul-filling wonder of this mysterious and miraculous night as the angel softly sings to our hearts the greatest of all Christmas songs: "Be not afraid; for behold, I bring you good news of great joy which shall be for all people (for you)—a living Savior and a true and eternal hope—Jesus Christ, the Lord." It is the heavenly host chorusing praise to God, making resonance in your body, soul, and spirit. It is bringing peace to inner strife, unity to inner chaos, light to inner darkness, holiness to our lust, love and joy to inner discontent and sorrow.

In this night, in this wonder of this heavenly Christmas, we can lose sight of our worldly want. We can shut our ears to the noises and distractions of the hustle and bustle of our daily living and fleshly needs and lusts; we can quiet the cries of our fears and sorrows that burrow deep within our soul. This sound and ability to hear does not reside in us naturally. It is our Lord Jesus who opens our ears and hearts for us as we simply—with purity, humility and contrition of heart—receive and cherish his gift of the life, love, peace, and joy of the babe in the manger.

Mary and Joseph got it. The shepherds got it. The world—Bethlehem, Jerusalem, the Roman Empire—missed it. They missed Christmas! They missed the Savior. Their lives were busy with religion, government and politics, social advancement, and personal idolatrous worship, just to name a few distractions that kept them from truly enjoying the freedom and life of "Christmas"—of Christ. What is it with you? What keeps you from missing Christmas? Let's not miss another Christmas, another day with Christ. Let us go to Jesus just as we are and bow down and worship. Then go and live your life rejoicing, glorifying, and praising God for all he has done, enjoying your life in his presence.

> Praise the Lord all nations; laud him, all peoples! For his lovingkindness is great toward us, and the truth of the Lord is everlasting. Praise the Lord.
>
> Psalm 117

The sound and experience of Christmas is supernatural. We cannot hear it with our own natural ears, nor experience it with our natural hearts. Do you want to hear and experience this gift? You won't experience it from anything created upon this earth. You will only experience it as you allow the Spirit's supernatural and miraculous touch to enter your heart and life. Are you with the shepherds who went away praising God for their delivery from the bondage of this flesh and fear to the redeeming love and security and freedom of the Savior? Are you with Mary, cherishing the reality of this heavenly gift of the Son of God? Do you ponder in your heart the wonder of God in you and His love and desire for you? He is right there awaiting your words of reception—to give you the heavenly sound and life of his *heavenly Christmas* miracle—his life to you! Yes, Lord, I believe and I receive.

&

"Father in heaven, how we long to hear the sound of Christmas, to hear the sound of your loving call and gift to us—the Lord Jesus crying out to us to come, to come to him and to receive life and purpose from him. Lead us, dear God, as you did the shepherds to the Babe in the manger. Lead us to that life. We come before you with grateful and humble hearts ready to receive your miracle of your heavenly Christmas, your life in ours. Thank you, my Lord and my God, my Savior, for this heavenly night, this heavenly sound, this heavenly calling to my life. I accept your gift of your life as I give my life in exchange. I believe your Christmas miracle. I believe your Christmas gift as I open it now and every day. Thank you, my Savior, for helping me hear the miracle and the wonder of a true heavenly Christmas. Amen and amen."

ౚ

My child, O how I wish I could be with you now and see you face to face. Do you ever think about this, this reality that some day we will see each other face to face (2Cor. 5:8; Phil. 1:23)? This will be a glorious day. Until that happens my hope for you is to keep this future as a vital hope in your life today. Your life on this earth, though fleeting, is full of trials and temptations. Keeping me in your heart, meditating on my life of love and truth for you will lift you out of the stress and entanglements of this world that prey on your vulnerable soul (Titus 2:13; John 14:1–3; 16:33; 1John 5:4).

Blessed are you when you meditate on me day and night. You will be like a tree firmly planted by streams of living water—my water of life (Ps. 1:-3). Blessed are you when you hunger and thirst for my righteousness for you will be satisfied to the full (Matt. 5:6). To meditate on me is to not waste time at all, but it is to make time to do all I have called you to do! Merry Christmas today and everyday my Christmas child. May you keep the sure hope of our meeting one day at the center of your heart, as I am doing.

Section Two

Christmas with Jesus

...I came that they might have life, and might have it abundantly.

John 10:10

Day Thirteen

You Are a Christmas Gift of Life!

☙

We are going to have some fun looking at some very special and wonderful gifts of Christmas the Lord has left for us to open. Actually, he has really not *left* us anything, as if he has gone away and said, "Good-bye, good luck. Hope you enjoy the gifts! Merry Christmas! Eat some pumpkin pie for me, and careful with the eggnog." He gives his gifts to us each and every day, for he is with us each and every day. We cannot separate his gifts from him. He desires for us to live in spiritual abundance of his life and gifts every day! He wants us to enjoy a full and joyful experience of his life and presence (and presents) in us. All we have to do is decide to take his gifts out of the "box," and with humble and grateful hearts, use them, enjoy them, and share them through the sharing of our lives in encouraging others with their truths.

Before we get to these life-changing, wonderful, and very useful gifts, let's talk just a bit more about Christmas and you and me, and how Christmas fits into our daily lives. Or, maybe I should say, how we should fit our lives into Christmas and the reason for the season—Jesus. Just like a child who cannot wait for Christmas to arrive and thinks that this time of the year is all about him or her (sad, but for the most part true), let us realize the truth that Christmas really is for you, although not in such a self-centered and greedy way as with a self-absorbed child perhaps, and maybe not in the way you might think. So snuggle up to one another, turn on the tree lights, put another log on the fire, light a Christmas candle or two (apple-pie or Christmas tree-scented of course), put some more popcorn in the popper. Of course do not forget the hot chocolate with a little drop of caramel and a pinch of cinnamon (Ali's family secret, hope Ali does not mind sharing this), and let us have some fun by simply first acknowledging to yourself that ... *you are a Christmas gift of life!*

Yes you are. No matter what you think about yourself, no matter where you find yourself, you are a Christmas gift. Believe it or not, you are a precious gift of the Lord (bought and paid for in advance–1Corinthians 6:20), and for the Lord as you give your life back to Him. You are a most precious and cherished gift the Author and Creator of your life will treasure forever. You are also a gift to others as he will use you in their lives in wondrous ways, as we will soon discover.

You are a gift—a Christmas gift of life given from the Lord to give back to him, then to others as he lives in and through you!

But right now you may not feel like a gift. You may feel like a lump of coal in the bottom of your Christmas stocking, perhaps. You might be living or maybe just existing and or surviving in one of two scenarios. Could either one of these two personal scenarios describe your life's routine?

Scenario Number One

Perhaps you are sitting in your office chair with a pile of stuff on your desk, around your desk, under your desk, and notes-to-self listed on little multicolored Post-it Notes plastered all over your computer screen, desk organizer, and even your body that scream out to you, "You *gotta* deal with this now!" Perhaps you are at home, tired of the rut and routine of doing the same old things over and over and over again. Maybe you are a student, a mechanic, a grocery clerk; maybe you are unemployed or involved with any number of jobs or positions in life that you let define who you are. You are wondering, "Isn't there more to life? Isn't there a better way? Just what am I doing here?" You are longing to feel significant, valued, appreciated; you hunger for love—a love that does not require anything in return. You are tired of playing the same old game of life—moving at a hundred miles per hour yet going nowhere, gaining no ground—or perhaps losing ground or getting buried under the rubble of your crumbling weaknesses and insecurities (kind of what happens at Christmastime?). In either case, you are definitely feeling tired and weary from your routine/rut, toil, and labor. You could very easily be bored, unchallenged, weary, and in a mental state of (shall we add some seasonal flavor) fruitcake and/or figgy pudding.

Or...

Scenario Number Two

You may be sitting pretty where you are. Life might be good. Finances are secure, relationships seem to be dependable, your plans and dreams are bathed in excitement and optimism, and you are even beginning to like your cat. You feel no real need or stress, your personal and professional conflict is low, and your life and soul is comfortable, for the moment anyway. You are in the small percentage of the population that could say, "I am ready for Christmas," when it is still two weeks away (how does that ever happen?). You feel good about yourself, life is exciting, and you look forward to whatever may come your way. "Bring it on," is your motto. You are ready.

Well... do not let either position in life fool you...

- or control you
- or lead you to think this is who you are
- or lead you to think there is no hope
- or lead you to think that you are your own hope

Let neither of these two scenarios, or any in between, define who you are. You are neither your riches nor your poverty (Luke 12:15; Proverbs 30:7–9). You are a specially created gift of the Lord: intently, intricately, intimately, and lovingly made and blessed with heavenly blessings (Psalm 139; Ephesians 1). Where you find yourself today—emotionally and physically—can and will change. And this change can happen by someone making a decision about you that you have no control over, without your consent or knowledge. Change can occur on a fleeting whim and fancy of an unchecked impulsive emotion, choice of attitude, or action by you or others. Change can occur due to a positive or negative word spoken. Your perspective and view of life can even change based on whether or not you have had a good meal, or as Ebenezer Scrooge has put it, "A bit of an undigested bit of beef, a blot of mustard, a crumb of cheese, a fragment of underdone potato."

Through any and all change, you are still the person God made you. The *real* you will not change, though you might perceive change as you let your circumstances control your reactions and even the thinking of who you are. Let us say you are an "A" student at the School of Gifts of the North Pole. Your talent and gifts are exemplified here in a joyful experience under the tutelage of Professor Claus and his myriad of elflike assistants (you like the assistants because they like to supply you with treats such as chocolate chip cookies and hot chocolate, that is, when the professor isn't watching ... and even when he is watching, for he too likes those little treats even more than you!). Needless to say, you are a solid "A" student simply because you truly enjoy the freedom you have of expressing the real you—there is no fear, only joy.

Unfortunately, you have to move away from this beautiful, inspiring, and soulful liberating wintry domain and head south (because there is no other direction to go in when you are at the North Pole). Your destination is the School of the Real World in Southern California (oh my). Because of your new and not comfortable environment you drop from being an "A" student to being a "C" student at best. Through this sliding transition your talents and gifts are squelched, even mocked and ridiculed, and your image of self goes further south than the physical move you had to make. You take all this in internally and feel terrible because the joy and innocent perspective you once had of yourself is now bathed in doubt and insecurity.

Has the true inner you changed, the you that God made you to be, or, have you just let the circumstances and where you are produce a surface change, even though you may feel great disturbances in your heart?

We cannot change the real individual God made us to be. What we do though, more often than not, is make a mess of our lives by living for self and the world instead of for our Maker and Christmas Savior. We let our culture and surroundings dictate to our hearts, who we are, why we are, what we think, the attitudes we choose, the emotions we let control us, and behaviors that come to define us by and through the priorities, principles, and eyes of the flesh and the world.

The "truth" is, you are more than what you perceive or what you feel, more than what the world makes you out to be; in a way, even more than what you are capable of thinking. In you, right where you are this Christmas season, is the potential to become all God desires you to be. His truth about you, his truth in you, and his truth for you has never changed. If I may say, you truly are his Christmas child, born as a gift to others and to himself— to be more of Christ in life.

You are his Christmas Gift!

❧

"Dear Christmas Savior, what a wonder you are. You have given your life for me so you could live your life through me. You have done this because of your great love and desire to make life worth living. This Christmastime I pray that I would learn a greater surrender of my life for you. Thank you for seeing me as your Christmas gift. Help me, Lord, to be a gift for others. As you live through me, let my life bring Christmas joy and good tidings to those in and around my life. Only you can do this. So because of this, I give my life back to you so you can use me for your glory and purpose. As Mary and Joseph prayed in surrendering their will to yours, I pray to be a vessel to do your bidding, just as you will, Lord, just as you will. Thank you, my Savior. Thank you for your gift of life in me. Jesus, it is in your name I pray."

Day Fourteen

Christmas Gifts from Above

℘

Blessed be the God and Father of our Lord Jesus Christ, who has blessed us with every spiritual blessing in the heavenly places in Christ.

Eph. 1:3

Merry Christmas, fellow *Christmastonians.* Christmas is a time of accentuated and exaggerated emotions and expectations to say the least. And this level of exaggerated Christmas emotions can even begin months before the Christmas season is upon us! Our pre-Christmas stress level can rise just by looking at gift ideas on the TV in August, receiving your first Christmas gift catalogue in September, seeing your first Christmas tree lot go up in the neighborhood right after the pumpkin patch people clean up the pumpkin patch mess, or hearing that first Christmas song in October (which is not necessarily a bad thing, although my family my disagree with me). Christmas can be a time when emotions can easily get a little heavy, thinking about missed friends or loved ones that are not present or have passed away. Feelings of loneliness and remorse over broken relationships and mistakes of the past play a big part in this time of Christmas.

Christmas can also have a strange and unexplainable influence on our perception of *time,* as *time* seems to run anxiously, if not painfully faster for some, or *excruciatingly* slower for others, depending on your personal circumstances and what you have to get done or wait for. In either case and all in between, the Christmas season does play havoc with whatever normalcy we have throughout the year.

Isn't it curious how Christmas can be a time of comfort, laughter, joy, and making merry to some; and at the same time, it can be so emotionally taxing and stressful on others? And how do the words, *anxious, stressful, taxing,* and *excruciating* enter into the picture of Christmas, a most wondrous and joyful time of the year?

I must make mention of this now before we enter into our gift opening spree. These words like *stress* and *anxiousness* enter into the picture of Christmas (and your everyday life) because of a simple yet profound exchange of priorities and principles. We exchange the Lord's priorities and principles, with which he established to bless our lives, with our fleshly/worldly life principles and priorities, which we have established and cling to, unwittingly destroying the peace, joy, purpose and contentment our Lord would have for us. We live exchanging the truth of God in and for our lives for the lies of our fleshy nature and culture. We think life is about us; thus, we live accordingly, like that self-absorbed child greedily wanting and waiting for all his Christmas booty. When in reality, life is about the source of Christmas, the reason for the season—Jesus. We have exchanged his priorities and principles and gift of his life with our own set of rules, values, and way of life. We have exchanged his selflessness and humility for our selfishness and boastful pride and arrogance, though we disguise these things with a false humility. We have neglected to open up and use his gifts of life, and instead have chosen to use what we think we have made for ourselves: our own talents, wisdom, strengths, and personalities.

So, what is Christmas about? We need to let the living Word tell us.

Christmas is about Jesus, plain and simple. Christmas is about the glory of God coming down upon us in the person of Jesus (Isaiah 7:14; 9:6; John 1:1–2, 14; 17: 1–5). Christmas is about Jesus and what he has done for us and what he has given to us, so that we can be poor of soul no longer (John 1:4, 29; 10:10; 3:16). He temporarily gave up his *rich* position in heaven to become *poor* in the flesh for us, that we might become *rich,* spiritually, in him (2 Corinthians 8:9). He came to be *born in the flesh* (what an amazing and incomprehensible and truly humbling concept), so that we could be *born of the Spirit* (John 3:3–7, 16).

Regardless of how you celebrate Christmas, regardless of where you celebrate Christmas, and regardless of whether or not you believe in the celebration and meaning of Christmas, there is an absolute and unshakable and immoveable truth that lies at the heart of life and at the heart of Christmas. This truth is Jesus Christ—the true and only reason for the Christmas season.

Christmas, though the word and chosen date of celebration is manmade, is a celebration that God is true. It is a celebration that God is a God of hope, love and grace and that he very much cares about his creation. Christmas is about a God who is just and holy, and because of his holiness and justice, he demands a price to be paid for the sinfulness of man. Sinful man in his natural sinful state (born in the flesh, separated from God) can have no personal relationship with a holy God. Man needs to be made holy himself - to be born of the Spirit (John 3:3). He needs to be reconciled to his heavenly Father (Romans 5:1,11; Colossians 1:20; Ephesians 2:1–3)! And this is where the beauty and true wonder of Christmas enters into the plan of redemption and gift of life from God for man. Christmas is about his unmerited and free gift of salvation. It is free for us because we cannot buy this gift; it is a gift bestowed to us from heaven (Ephesians 2:8–9; Romans 6:23). There is absolutely nothing we can do to merit such a gift.

All we can do is accept this gift freely given to us (John 3:16; Acts 4:12; 16:31; Romans 6:23; 10:9–10; Isaiah 5:1–3).

The definition of a gift is that it is free, given of a free will, accepted by free will. It is given once and for all (Jude 3; Romans 6:10; Hebrews 9:28; 1 Peter 3:18). Though there is nothing we can do to buy this gift of eternal life, it does cost us something. It cost us our own life, picking up that instrument of death—the cross—and following Jesus (Mark 8:34–38). Listening to, trusting in, and obeying the Savior of the world in following his ways and no longer our own (1 John 2:4, 6; 5:2–3) leads us to his abundant life he so desires for us (John 10:10; Psalm 37:4; 145:8–9, 14–16).

The meaning and celebration and the truth and gift of Christmas cost God, his Son (Romans 8:3). To him our salvation was not free, but in fact very costly. The incarnation, Immanuel (Isaiah 7:14; John 1:14), is something we cannot fully understand. He came to endure the trials of fallen man in pain and hunger, in suffering and temptation, and ultimately death, so we might have victory through him over all these things (John 16:33; 1 Corinthians 10:13; 15:56; 1 John 5:4). He endured all he did without grumbling, or sin, yet with joy—Christmas joy, shall we say.

Do you want to understand the true joy of Christmas? This is it. Jesus, for the joy set before him endured the cross for us because of his love for us (Hebrews 12:2). This is the true joy of Christmas, to receive and then to share this truly remarkable sacrificial gift. The joy of Christmas is not necessarily in what we do during this time of the year, but what has already been done for us by Jesus Christ. What we do for one another can bring happiness, but the true *Christmas joy* can only come from the heart of Jesus in our hearts as we give him the gift of our life and live and love the way he did and does for us. *Christmas happiness* is brought about and manufactured by external things, and there can be great fun and sharing of lives in these things. *Christmas joy* is brought about by internal things—the sharing of our hearts with Jesus, and his with ours. Man's *Christmas happiness* is fleeting and can often turn into anything but happiness, i.e., stress, greed, loneliness and despair. *Christmas joy* is eternal and can only turn our temporal and fickle happiness into a true and greater joy as we allow the true meaning of Christmas—Jesus—to live in our hearts as his true heavenly gift of Christmas.

ఇం

"My Christmas Savior and gift of life, may you be blessed and your name lifted up high throughout the world today and always. May you, gracious Lord, be glorified in my life and in this Christmas season. Thank you for all you have done and are doing. Thank you for family and friends, for provision and protection. Thank you for the thousands and thousands of life's blessings and gifts you so faithfully bestow upon me that sadly, I so ungratefully do not even acknowledge, use, or appreciate. Help me see this in a new way, Lord. Turn my heart back to you; turn my eyes back to you to see who you are, to see and hear your true Christmas miracle and wonder. I have been blind to your Christmas wonder and life because of my selfish ways. Lord, I lay all my life at your feet and only look forward to communing with you once again. Merry Christmas, Jesus my Savior. May my gift of my life be acceptable in your sight. Receive my gift, Lord, with open and loving arms because you are the only one I can trust to take my life and guard it and cherish it with your eternal Christmas heart of love and holiness and perfect compassion. Thank you, my Savior. Thank you."

Day Fifteen

the Gift of My Image—a New Identity

&

Therefore if any man is in Christ, he is a new creature; the
old things passed away; behold, new things have come.

2Cor. 5:17

The first and glorious Christmas morn, the day of our
Savior's birth, is the only foundation man has for his
new birth of a new life (John 3:3, 16; 14:6). Jesus came to
give his life as a gift—an offering of sacrifice to his Father so he
could give us new life in the Son. Without this gift of the Son,
we would have no true life. Jesus says, *In me you have life and as
you abide in me I will produce fruit in you. But if you do not abide in
me, you do not have life and no fruit or gifts could I produce through
you or for you* (John 15; Galatians 5:22–23).

Within this gift of his life *in us,* there are many unopened
gifts—gifts we rarely acknowledge and appreciate. The phrase
"in you" (Colossians 1:27) is the premise for these gifts. Because
his life is *in us,* we are far more than we think we are. We are
more than what we wear, what we see on the outside, and even
what we are aware of on the inside. We are more than what we

own, what our status or position might be, and certainly what the world of others think about us. Because he is in us we have access to his wisdom, mind, heart, vision, insight, strength, heavenly riches, hope, peace, joy and love.

Let's look at just twelve of these gifts and joyfully receive these gifts by appreciating them, and then putting them into action in our own lives by sharing them with those in and around our lives.

So, what did you ask for Christmas? C'mon, what was on your list? Was it some article of clothing you thought you would look good in? Was it a hobby item that would help add to your expertise in making things? How about a book to grow spiritually or to further enlighten or entertain at a personal level? Many if not all of our "Christmas-listed" items most likely fit us; that is, they are about who we think we are, or what we think makes us who we are—they are about self. Let us with gleeful and anticipatory excitement look under our Christmas tree—in the life of Jesus—to spy something new, if not unexpected, that we can fully enjoy; and as well, let us use these gifts to change our lives today through forevermore.

"Who am I?" is the hidden strain of our heart. The world says, "You are what you eat." "You are what you wear." "You are what you do." "You are what you drive, possess, or have achieved," or, "You are what you think." The bottom line to this worldly way of thinking is, "You are what you can do for yourself: what you think about yourself on the inside, and in what you can make yourself look like on the outside." This assessment of a positive or negative self-identity/image comes from the eyes of your own mind and heart (Proverbs 18:10–12) strongly influenced by how you think you are seen through the eyes of the world! Personally, I do not think we should trust either of these two sources—self or the world (Psalm 118:8–9; Jer. 17:9; 1Cor. 1:18–30).

ও

"Oh my Lord, I can easily get so confused about who I really am. I hear the many voices in the world: voices from friends and coworkers, voices at school, at my workplace, from the scores of books and inspirational speakers all telling me, "This is who I was; this is who I am; this is who I can be." I get labeled according to my personality, my emotional drive and condition, my intellect, my passion, and zeal. I get labeled because of my past, my potential, my possessions, and position in career and life, my family history, or the way I look, the color of my skin, or the accent of my tongue. My spouse sees me as a spouse; my children see me as a parent; my coworkers see me as a coworker; my employer as an employee, and vice-versa; my socializing buddies see me as a buddy. They all see me and would define me in different ways as to who I am. I often keep all these opinions separate or compartmentalized. Is it any wonder I can be confused as to who I really am?

"Dear Savior, I look in the mirror and I am not sure I see what you see. I see the reflection of my flesh, the color of my hair, the skin on my face and the imperfections on my body. The physical vision can so easily be skewed from reality as you see me and know me to be. I may see beauty when others see, well, let's be honest and say, ugly, or vice-versa. I may see skinny or fat while others see the opposite. I may see muscles, and others may do their best to hold in a laugh. And should I take such a courageous look inside, I see my inner soulful strengths, weaknesses, and maladies. I see my sin and memories that bind me to the past; my sinful attitudes, emotions, insecurities, and thoughts that strangle out the joy of today and the worries and fears of tomorrow that seem to keep me imprisoned and wed to my limited sin-tainted heart's perspective and vision.

"Oh, Lord, as I take this internal and external look of myself, not only do I see through my own tainted and clouded vision of a prideful and vain heart or of an arrogance of false humility and self-pity, I see them through the lens of what others say and think about me. All these things seem to so relentlessly control me. My Lord, this is hardly the truth I need to live freely and joyfully in you. What I need is your truth and your opinion of me. I need to know not my own self-image and identity, but your image and identity for me.

"May you this Christmas season help me open your wonderful gift of my true identity in you. For I am sorely tired and weary of judging myself based on what the world of friends and even family say about me, and how I let the images of Hollywood and the advertisers of Market Street convince me of who I am and who I need to be. Help me, Lord, take my eyes off the external physical image I see, and even the lies and misconceptions I believe about myself internally, to see the true image of who I am created to be in you."

୪

My beautiful Christmas child, you are beautiful to me, regardless of what you or others think about yourself. Merry Christmas this morning and every morning for the rest of your life. You are beautiful to me.

I see your heart wanting to be accepted and wanting to be loved simply because of who you are. I see your heart putting itself out there wanting to be valued and appreciated for the things you do. I also see your heart trying to puff itself up through accomplishments proving to yourself and the world that you are better than who you and they think you are. And I see your heart crushed in disappointment, in suffering and pain because the world and your own flesh has turned against you, saying you are not good enough, you are not pretty enough, you are not talented enough, you are not smart enough, you simply are not adequate. I also see a world that wants to deceive you and seductively lure you in to its lair, only to tear you up with its razor-sharp teeth of judgment and condemnation (1 Peter 5:8; John 10:10).

Rest yourself in me and find your true identity of the full person I created you to be. Incline your ear and come to me, listen that you may live and find the fullness of me within you (Prov. 2:1–5, 8:32–36; Isa. 55:3; Eph. 3:19)

&

My child, you are my wondrous creation (Psalm 139:14); my work of poetry (Ephesians 2:10); you are the apple of my eye (Psalm 17:8). I have created you in the image of myself (Genesis 1:27). What is better than this? I tell you, nothing. You have striven long enough to fit into the mold and image of the world. You have lived long enough living in the foolishness and lusts of the flesh (1 Peter 4:3). You have lived long enough looking into the mirror of vanity. You have lived long enough listening to everybody in your world, including your prideful self, instead of listening to me. Turn to me (1 Peter 4:2), accept my gift to you as being created in my image, made perfectly, fearfully, and intently (Psalm 139:13–15). I sculpted you with my own hands. I formed you in your mother's womb. I have made you to reflect my image on the inside for my glory.

Leave this world of comparison behind from this day forward. Look not to the world for comparison or standards of what you have or do not have, what you look like, or what you wear. Tying your heart to this world you will only bind and twist yourself into an ungodly image that does not reflect me, but reflects the wickedness of this world. Tying your heart to this world and trying to meet the standards that are worldly and fleshly mean absolutely nothing to me and will be ultimately destructive to you.

The world and the "god of this world" will want to rob you of this gift of your true identity because it is this gift that is so valuable to me (John 10:10; 2 Corinthians 4:4). I have made you wonderful and I do not make mistakes—you are beautiful! The devil will use and abuse this gift against you because there is great weakness here in your flesh. Your vanity is so volatile to your sensitive fleshly life, producing great emotional vulnerability, stress and pain. When you allow the world to make you sad and become burdened in this area of your identity, you become lost and insecure and miserable, and it is hard for my light and life to shine in you and through you as my child—the child I intend for you to be.

Just as a young child with childlike simplicity and purity trusts themselves to their parents, so I want you to do this with me. Children of innocence and purity of heart do not have a self-consciousness of what they look like and what the world thinks of them. I want you to lose your self-consciousness about these things and have only a Christ-consciousness. Believe it or not, this is possible, but it is only possible as you let go of your self-image and self-consciousness and trust me for your life and identity.

Look to me, my child, and be radiant (Psalm 34:5). Look to me and be miserable no more (Psalm 42:5). Open my gift of your new identity and let your heart be free to rejoice in the wonder of who you are in me. Let the world see me in you and see you for the wondrous creation I have made you to be. Because that is exactly what you are—my wondrous creation of my own hands! Your ears, eyes, nose, hands, and toes were all created by me and can be and will be used for me (1 Corinthians 12)! Your identity is not in what you do; it is not in what you look like; it is not in what you possess or in the name you have perhaps made for yourself. Your identity is only found in me, and as you rest in me, I will live through you so people will see not your physical image or your accomplishments or title, but the radiance of my glory shining through you (Ps. 34:5).

Next time you look in the mirror, do not look at the reflection and let that dictate your disposition of thought, emotions, and attitudes for this day. This mirror only distorts and perverts the real you into an ugly monster of pride and self-centered vanity and idolatry. You are looking at this reflection through your eyes of the flesh and not through my eyes of the Spirit. Let me give you this gift of my mirror of my character and of my truth to show you your true reflection of who you really are in me.

Merry Christmas, my child, for that is who you are—you are my beautiful child, bearing my name, with my Spirit within you so I might live my life through you. You are a new creature with a new purpose (2 Corinthians 5:17). This is who you are. Can you think of anything greater than this?

∞

"My Wondrous Creator, divert my eyes from this world of falsely satisfying images of vanity and pride. Direct my eyes to the true image and reality of you. Thank you, Lord Jesus, for being my true identity. Thank you for making me in your image, for imparting to me your righteousness (2 Corinthians 5:21), for blessing me with your unfathomable and unmerited and amazing love (Romans 5:8; 8:37–39; John 3:16). I am found in you. I am not what I see or the world sees; I am who I am because you are who you are in me. Help me see myself this way, gracious Savior. Help me lose myself—all that negative emotionally charged perception of who I am—in the beauty of you and your wondrous calling of my life to you. Thank you, my gracious Gift-Giver. Thank you for giving me this new gift of my identity on this Christmas day."

Day Sixteen

The Gift of my Heart—a New Purpose

ॐ

For we are His workmanship, created in Christ Jesus for good works, which God prepared beforehand, that we should walk in them.

Eph. 2:10

Rudolph the red-nosed reindeer had a very shiny nose … We all know this charming little Christmas story. Rudolph goes from an unwanted misfit not knowing where or how he fits into his culture of family and friends, to being the hero of Christmas, at least, Christmas at the North Pole as the story goes.

Rudolph was "born" with a very unique and soon to be discovered and appreciated special, shining, glowing, illuminating, storm and darkness of "peanut butter" piercing Red nose. At first he didn't know where he fit in. His friends shunned him—they would not let him play in any of their reindeer games—and his parents tried to hide his, shall we say, hard to hide imperfection. Life was not a happy life for Rudolph as he tried to escape to

Misfit Island, where all the misfit toys went to spend their misfit lives.

It wasn't until a terrible storm hit the North Pole, on Christmas Eve no less, when Santa was ready to hit the emergency stop button, canceling Christmas due to the darkness of the storm of all storms. Well, you know the story. Santa realized that Rudolph with his glowing and beaconing shining red nose could easily light the way through the darkness for him to deliver his sleigh full of goodies to children around the world. This Christmas for Rudolph was a Christmas of discovery as he (and his friends) realized a new and wonderful purpose for his rather unusual and special gift. When once he thought his nose was a curse and his life was perhaps rather useless, now he sees his life as a purposeful blessing for everybody. When once he felt very purposeless, he realized how purposeful he really could be!

Now, to go from fantasy to real life may not be as difficult a stretch as you might think, especially when one factors in the Maker of all storm-stopping miracles in the formula. Maybe like Rudolph you feel you do not fit in and are wondering these common to mankind questions:

"What is my purpose in life?"

"What is God's will for my life?"

"How do I know if I should take this job, make this move, marry this person … or something as trivial as, what color car should I buy, or should I get a dog or a cat or a bird, or a reptile?'

Been there, asked that? Worried about these questions? These are just a few questions we ask ourselves as we try to figure life out "under the sun," as King Solomon might phrase it.

Do you know one thing that really throws confusion into our already confused and scattered lives as we try to figure out our purpose? It is the way and philosophy of life in this world that teaches us to compartmentalize our lives. The way our lives are scattered into so many fragments of doing this or doing that, we naturally tend to see our lives in many different arenas or compartments. Our lives may be divided up into a job or career compartment, a parental or a child compartment, a church service compartment, a private time with the Lord or God compartment, or a social, entertainment, or hobby compartment. The list of compartments go on and on and differ from individual to individual. The point is we are somewhat *scattered*, internally and externally because of how we have unintentionally set up these compartments. When we go into a certain compartment, we drop who we were in the last compartment and put on who we are supposed to be in the next compartment. Thus, without much effort, we divide our thoughts, objectives, dreams, and purpose between these compartments with little integration between them. There is great disconnect within our self.

We live in this compartmentalized state of being—not very together, not very much at peace, and not very directed with a common theme or purpose in our divided yet singularly whole lives. This is especially true as we so easily define "secular" and "spiritual" compartments to our lives. Because of the reality of these many compartments, is it any wonder why we fail at discerning a true purpose for our lives? Is it any wonder that we might be so frustrated and weary physically, emotionally and spiritually?

॰ஐ॰

"My King and my Lord, the wonder of the Christmas season and life, I am lost and without your true purpose in my life right now. Though I am doing things, I feel I am really going nowhere. I am not sure that what I am doing is of any value to anybody, including myself and especially you. I look to the future and am not sure where I want to be, or should be, or should do, even at an age that equals four or five times my shoe size. My dreams and aspirations that I once thought admirable even possibly in your will for me, I am now not sure anymore.

"Oh, my Savior, may you bring me together today, Lord. May you unite my life in your life and purpose for me. I am too scattered with the many things I think are important to me, with the many things I think I need to do to make my life purposeful and to make my life work. I need your help in discerning how I have compartmentalized my life and most importantly how this compartmentalization has kept you at a distance from working out your purpose in every area of my life. I do feel scattered Lord. I need you and your unifying wisdom and life that you might be glorified in my life for your good pleasure (Philippians 2:13). Lord, teach me your way; I will walk in your truth; Lord, unite my heart, my inner being to fear Thy name (Psalm 86:11); bring my life together with your purpose and identity in me and for me."

ઉ

Merry Christmas my dear one, with too many toys, too many thoughts, too many distractions within and around your life. You are wondering just what your purpose is? Well, first realize and know this. I have not made and purposed you to necessarily to be Larry the loving spouse, or Cathy the coolest mom, or Garrett the greatest brother, or Simon the smartest scientist, or Tina the tennis player. I have made you and purposed you for a very high calling (Phil. 3:14). It is first to be my child (John 1:12) and to love me with all your heart, mind, soul, and with all your strength (Matthew 22:37; Deuteronomy 6:5). I want you to be devoted to me, simply and purely with great joy (2 Corinthians 11:3; Matt. 10:37–42). This is when your life works best. This purpose of being my child is to simply enjoy growing up in my kingdom, with me being your heavenly king, parent, and friend (Matthew 6:9; John 15:14–15; Galatians 4:6–7). Your purpose is to walk in and reflect my holiness (1 Peter 1:15–16). This is what your life is about. Trust me to guide your life and provide all your needs for you (Philippians 4:19; 2 Timothy 3:16–17; Matthew 6:33; Ps. 55:22). For what parent would neglect their own child (Hebrews 12:7; Matthew 7:9)? Let us grow together this way every day of your life here on earth and with me eternally by your side.

I have purposed you to let me live through you (Galatians 2:20). I have purposed you to serve me this way (Romans 12:1). Remember the words of the Spirit as he wrote through Paul that you are no longer your own, but that I have bought you and that you are to glorify me (1 Corinthians 6:19)? This is best done as you allow me to live through you (John 15). In doing this, you walk with me to work out your salvation for my pleasure (Philippians 2:12–13; Eph. 5:1).

I have purposed you also to endure some suffering, so please do not be surprised when suffering and persecution come your way. Know that through this I will be glorified, if you allow me to (1 Peter 2:21, 3:14, 4:1). I do not want you to suffer in the ways of the world (1Pet. 4:14–16), but in this world as you follow me, you will have to endure some suffering, but fear not (John 16:33), even in this there is great purpose and peace if your suffering is for me (Hebrews 12:10–11). I will comfort you (2Cor. 1:3–4).

I have purposed you to be my ambassador and representative to this fallen and needy world (2 Corinthians 5:18–20; Matt. 5:13–16). I have called you to go out and make disciples (Matthew 28:18–20). Your friend or neighbor has a need. I want you to go meet that need (Luke 10:30–37; Galatians 6:2). I have called you to be my hands, feet, mouth, and ears. Be me to one who needs me, even though they do not see this need or even when they turn their backs on me by turning their backs on you.

You wonder what your purpose is and you look to find your purpose in the things and ways of the fleshly world. You will not find your purpose this way. Yes, I have called you and purposed you to work in this world, but I have not called you to be *of* this world or to become like the world (Colossians 3:1–3; 1 John 2:15; 1 Peter 1:15). You may have a very fine and lucrative career, but this is not your purpose or calling. You may be struggling to find work, but this does not define my calling upon your life. You may be learning and growing to make a certain profession your livelihood, but this is not necessarily your purpose. You may be a leader or involved in community, even church programs and ministries, but these, too, may not necessarily be your purpose or calling.

In all that you do, whether it be a spouse, parent, friend, businessman, etc., live for me so I can live through you in all these areas. The world will no longer define you in these ways, but I will define you and bless you in all you do. Live for me so I can live through you in all areas of your life. In doing this you will no longer feel scattered or compartmentalized.

Please know I can and will use wherever you are for my purpose and glory, even though you may see your present position as useless. Joseph and Paul were in prison; David was a shepherd boy; Moses spent forty years in the back side of the desert; Rahab was a harlot; Jesus hung on a cross. Please know that in my sovereignty I will make all things work out for my good (Romans 8:28). I must bring this back to a foundational truth and necessity. Your purpose in life is not to try to fulfill what you think your purpose is. It is to come to me as a child (Matthew 11:28; 18:3), a willing servant, making your body a willing and holy sacrifice (Romans 12:1–2), to take off your own yoke of self-importance—fleshly slavery—and put on my yoke and learn from me (Matthew11:2). Let me lead you on the path of my desired purpose and abundance for your life (Psalm 37:4-).

Merry Christmas, my dearest. Let me give you this

never-ending gift of my holy purpose and provision for your life each and every day.

෩

"Dear God, turn my thoughts of what I think is important to what you know to be important for my life. I often get so lost as I try to make my own way in living my life as I think you would. Lord, often I end up frustrated and weary because I think I am doing what you want me to do, only to find out my motives and effort have been self-centered. May your Spirit renew me in your purpose with your motive in your strength guiding me to a new life, starting today. I am realizing that this Christian life is not so much about doing, though I joyfully and willingly obey your words, but it is more about being and resting in you. My purpose is not what I can do in this world, but about who I am in you. You are my ultimate purpose. You are the end of my searching for fulfillment and accomplishment. It is only as I empty myself of self I can be full of your life and purpose for me. It is only after I die to self that you can live through me. It is only after I surrender my all that you can be all in and through me. What greater purpose can there be than this? There can be none. You are my purpose. Thank you for such a wonderful Christmas and everyday gift. May I realize and use this gift for your glory with every step I take."

Day Seventeen

The Gift of Spiritualities—Spiritual Gifts

&

Now there are varieties of gifts, but the same Spirit. And there are varieties of ministries, and the same Lord. And there are varieties of effects, but the same God who works all things in all persons. But to each one is given the manifestation of the Spirit for the common good.

1 Cor. 12:4–6

Look at your Christmas tree. It is made up of a trunk, branches, and needles, right? That is at least what you can see on the outside. Internally there are many more things that make up the tree. You just cannot see them at the cellular level. On your Christmas tree there are ornaments, lights, popcorn, tinsel, and perhaps many other traditional decorations. These are all in different colors, shapes, sizes, and luminosity. Take one type of decorations away and the Christmas tree would be lacking something you have desired it to look like. If you were to have just one kind of decoration, your tree might look kind of boring, some might think. Or what if your tree was just a trunk, or just a branch, or just one big needle? Where would you hang all those Christmas decorations? Your Christmas tree would not be much of a Christmas tree, would it?

Listen to a traditional rendering of a Christmas favorite, "Sleigh Ride." In this musical piece you can hear many different types of horns and different types of percussion instruments. You can hear flutes and clarinets, violins and other stringed instruments as well. You even hear a whip and a cowbell of sorts. If any one instrument were to play its part alone, you would not be able to hear the *wonderful whole* as originally intended and designed. Even if you heard two, or three, or four instruments together you would still not get the desired result. The song would certainly be missing something. It would not be complete. It is not until all the instruments come together and play their own specifically designed parts, all the while following the conductor, would you hear the symphonic wonder as it was meant to be.

So it is with the wonderfully and specifically crafted organism of the body of Christ. The Church—his body, is made up of many diverse, uniquely, and intricately designed and purposed individuals—you and me—all for the purpose of lifting up the glorious song of praise to the name of the Orchestrator, the Conductor and Composer of all life, Jesus! We need to all work together as the Lord purposed us for the building up of itself for the purpose of reaching the world with the awesome sound of the wonder of a *heavenly Christmas* praising his name, the Savior of the world, Jesus.

ॐ

"Dear Lord, dear Spirit, the Distributor and Enabler of your gifts in the Church and in me, may you continue to do your mighty work in accomplishing your purposes. I would pray that you lead me to the knowledge and discernment of knowing just what spiritual gifts you have for me. Lord, thank you for these gifts and the passion you have put into my heart. Thank you for desiring to use me in such a special way in being part of your orchestrated plan in the life I am now living.

"But Lord, I must confess, there is part of me that feels fearful and lazy, and I find it hard to get involved. I guess I am still so very selfish about my own life and time. I am fearful about being rejected or failing or making a fool of myself. I often feel that I am not good enough, or I am too entangled in some sin. Lord, there are times, like most of the time, I feel I have nothing to offer. And, Lord, at times (again like most of the time), I feel I have so much other "stuff" I have to do that I just do not have time for this commitment. To be more honest, I do not know if I want to make time to serve you and the Church this way. In my heart though, I really do believe that I want to serve you. I need your encouragement with this. I need your help, my Savior.

છ

My Christmas child, if you only knew the wonderful plans I have for you (John 10:10; Eph. 2:10; Jeremiah 29:11). If you only knew how blessed you would feel if you just trusted me in this area of your life. I must tell you I have created you and blessed you with a unique ability to be used in my body—the Church. And I want you to know that the gifts and talents I have instilled in you are perfect for you. It might be to teach or provide encouragement and counsel. It might be to serve or be a leader of a ministry. You might have a desire to simply give above and beyond your tithe. There are many gifts I have for my body. Continue in your prayers about this and let me show you your gifts and your passion and your strengths that can be of use to me. Let me encourage you to seek out counsel to help you discern just what I am showing you and how I have given to you.

You do not need to be afraid of wasting time, or committing your time, or feel like you do not belong or have nothing to offer. Do not be afraid of failing or of what others may think. And please do not think your have to be perfect before I can use you. As you walk with me, I promise I will bless your Christmas stockings off the mantle of your fearful and stubborn heart with purpose and value you have never felt before.

Do not seek these gifts with prideful intent or selfish use, but with humility and confidence in me, let me show you, then use your gifts for my glory and the building up of my Church (James. 4:1–4; 1 Corinthians 12:7, 25; Ephesians 4:12). Just as I have given you gifts to bless others, others have gifts from me to bless you. This is how I have made the body to work. Please do not compare yourself with anybody else. Realize, I may have made you to be a piccolo for wonderful melodic highlights in my symphony of life, while another may be the French horn. Though much more bold and loud, it has its own unique and important contribution quite different from yours. Though each distinct, each is equally important and valuable.

You will never feel a more full experience of life and joy, of purpose and peace than when I use you as you were designed. If you have a sense that something is missing in your life, this could be a big piece of the puzzle. I have made you for this purpose and until you allow me to show you how and why I made you in this way, you will feel somewhat empty. Nobody has a more important role to play than you. Different roles, yes, more upfront or leading roles, perhaps, but every individual that comprises my body is essential and vital, this includes you (1 Corinthians 12). To make my Church, and your life work the way it pleases me, everybody must work together under my purpose and leading and strength (Ephesians 4:1–6).

Merry Christmas, my wonderful and unique

Christmas gift. May you accept my gift to you and let me say thank you for accepting and using my gift to make this day and every day the merriest and joyous Christmas musicals and symphonies of life and Christmas celebrations.

ဢ

"Dearest Giver of eternal gifts from above, may you be pleased to hear from your child now. Thank you, wonderful and mysterious Orchestrator of life. What a mystery is the working of your body—the Church here on earth. Thank you for gifting me with your life, your wisdom, and your purposeful gifts in making me complete. Thank you, Lord, for making me unique for the purpose and edification and building up of your Body. Use me for your purpose and all for your glory."

Day Eighteen

the Gift of my Confidence—the Presence of the Holy Spirit

෩

If you love Me, you will keep My commandments. And I will ask the Father, and He will give you another Helper, that He may be with you forever, that is the Spirit of truth ...

John 14:15–17

Though a host encamp against me, my heart will not fear; though war arise against me, in spite of this I shall be confident.

Ps. 27:3

The story of Santa Claus can be a wonderful and charming little story. The thought of a stout and rosy-cheeked cherub-type fellow, quite mystical and whimsical, loading up his sleigh one night a year and distributing gifts and good cheer is captivating, if not enrapturing. Children of all ages have fun with this jolly and round 'ole fellow wearing his Santa's attire, with gold buttons no less. The excitement in children's hearts on

Christmas Eve is overflowing as they anticipate the arrival of Santa that winter's night eve. It seems that the cares of the world disappear on this one particular night as the magic of Santa coming to visit us on Christmas fills the heartfelt imaginations of many throughout the world.

But what about the real source and focus of Christmas? Not magic, but miracle; not Santa, but the Savior; not just a gift giver, but the gift himself?

There is a closing line in a favorite Christmas song that goes like this: "The hopes and fears through all the years are met in Thee tonight." This line is from "O Little Town of Bethlehem," and the words are referring not to the one-night-a-year-visiting Santa, but to the true gift giver, the Savior, Jesus Christ the Lord, who is with us now and forevermore.

&

"My Savior, I walk through this life unsure of so many things. It seems that as soon as I take my eyes and my heart's focus off you I find myself lost in a tailspin of emotions and indecision. Like Peter on the water walking toward you, he started to sink as he was distracted by the storm around him and the impossibility of what he was doing. His confidence was in you for one moment in obeying your call to get out of the boat and walk, and then the next moment, his confidence was back on himself in pride or fear, which led to a fall into the turbulent sea of fear and doubt. In his pride Peter might have said to himself, "Hey, look what I am doing. I must be pretty special," thinking it was actually himself that was making this miracle work. And then in a blink, fear and doubt entered in as he saw in his weak flesh the impossibility of the moment, "What am I doing? This is not possible!"

"Lord, this world and my flesh call to me. It screams to me to trust and rely on only myself. The world of sight teaches me to trust in only that which I can see, touch, understand, and control (2 Peter 3:1–4; 2:1–3; 2 Timothy 3:1–7). It tries to convince me not to be confident in a "religion" that from the world's point of view is subjective and illogical. The world's teaching and philosophies may not be so bold to say it out loud that there is no God (Psalm 10:3–4; 14:1), but with subtlety it would have me question your word, your intent, your character and person (like in the Garden with Eve, Genesis 3:1–5). Then when this is rooted in my soul, faith that you require (Hebrews 11:6; 1–2) begins to seem so very unreasonable and illogical, if not impossible. The ways of the flesh and world and the "god of this world" tell me to not trust and believe in a God whom I cannot see or fully understand, but to put my confidence in my own mind and strength, that which I can see and understand, and control.

"Lord, you know far more than I how untrustworthy this world of flesh is, yet I so struggle with letting go of the world of flesh because quite simply, 'I want to be in charge' (Proverbs 16:18, 25). You know how many times I have fallen and been led into entanglements by following and putting confidence in the world of things and my fleshly priorities and philosophies (Luke 15:12–16). Help me, Lord, this Christmastime, to let go of this confidence of the flesh and of my own way of thinking and to truly put my confidence in you (2Cor. 3:5. 4:7). Help me to see in a new way how you entrusted everything to the Father and did nothing of or for yourself. As you saw the Father doing, so you did. His will was your will. Lord, You alone are my confidence, just as the Father was your confidence when you walked in my shoes of weak flesh. You alone are my confidence as I try to walk in your shoes, in the Spirit. Your good word says, *in the fear of the Lord there is strong confidence, and his children will have refuge* (Prov. 14:26). Help me understand what it is to greater fear you; help me grow in confidence, not in my flesh but in your presence that I might rest and be secure in your heart—my refuge. Help me see this gift of your presence—the marvelous and awesome Holy Spirit, as my confidence in life in a new and vital way (Matthew 28:20; Acts 1:8).

ॐ

I am with you, my Christmas child. I am with you always and until the end of this life and beyond (Psalm 48:14). I am your confidence. I am the reason you can go though the storms of life in peace (Psalm 23:4; Mark 4:37–40; 6:48–51). When you go to work, to school, or to play each day and you are not sure what awaits you, guess what? I will be with you. When you have an appointment or there is something you may not want to do but have to do, guess what? I am there with you. When you are deep in a trial or test, when your emotions are raw and ragged because of some disturbing news, when you see all the evil and violence in this world arriving on your doorstep, guess what? I will never leave your side (Psalm 18:6–19; 27:1–3; Isaiah 41:10–13).

You may want to fit into the world to gain acceptance or be appreciated or feel you are worth something. Do not go there (1 John 2:15; James 4:4; Luke 12:15). I am your confidence (Psalm 16:8). You may feel frantically desperate, drowning in a sea of stress, turmoil, and a life out of control. Fear not, I am with you, and I am in perfect control. I am all you need (Matthew 6:33; Daniel 11:32; Philippians 4:13, 19). You may attempt to do something new, something out of your comfort zone; you may be asked to do something that scares you. I encourage you to change your perspective, and do not look at the fear and possibility of failure or embarrassment, but take a deep breath of my Spirit, smile, and let me be your confidence (Hebrews 12:2; Psalm 73:25–26).

I must say that it is only me that you live to please. Though you may think it is important to gain approval and praise from man, this is only a lure of the flesh to feed the flesh, thus squelch my life in you. I am your only audience, in this there is great comfort and security. There is nothing that man can do to you that I cannot take care of (Psalm 56). I have lived in your shoes (Hebrews 4:15; 2:18) so you do not have to fear your shoes wearing out with worry or fear as you walk this earth, if you walk in me. I have overcome all temptations so you do not have to worry and fear facing any trial by yourself (John 16:33; 1 Corinthians 10:13; Hebrews 2:18, 4:15). As you make me your confidence, you will come forth as gold (1 Peter 1:7; 1 Corinthians 10:13)! Do not put any confidence in your flesh. Put all confidence—your faith—in me (John 15:5; Philippians 3:3; John 6:63). Let go of fearing the world of men and their ways to control you, for if I am with you what can man do to you (Psalm 56)? Know that your life is in me and I am in you, and I am in sovereign control over all (Colossians 3:1–3; Psalm 103:19). With this knowledge, move forward with confidence (Hebrews 4:16) in my strength and wisdom. I will faithfully and lovingly guide you every step of the way as you allow me to (Proverbs 3:5–6; 28:26).

You have the power and life of the Holy Spirit in you (Acts 1:8; 1 Corinthians 3:16; 6:19–20). The Spirit gives you power to take control of your thoughts (1Corinthians 2:16; Philippians 4:8–9; 2 Timothy 1:7). You have the power to not sin, be enslaved to sin or be overcome by temptation (1 Corinthians 10:13). You have the power to walk by faith and not by sight (2 Corinthians 5:7; Hebrews 11:6; 12:2; Matthew 14:28–29). You have the power to learn from me, be directed by me, to be my witness where I lead you (John 14:16, 26; Matthew 28:19–20). You have the power to give up living for yourself and to truly live for me (Philippians 3:8–14).

Merry Christmas, my Christmas child. May you be overwhelmed in my presence today as you choose to set aside the alluring and glittering packages this world and the flesh has to offer. Let go of the hold onto your flesh in all its pride and weaknesses and stubbornness for independence and self-reliance. Let go of your life and with my presence in your life, which is your confidence, live every moment of every day reveling in this gift of the power and life of the Holy Spirit. Let my presence and this present be your soulful confidence. My Spirit will lead you, teach you, comfort you, counsel you, and in love convict and encourage you in my love and holiness throughout your life!

డ

"Dear Spirit, how wonderful it is when I finally and truly surrender to you. Please forgive me for so stubbornly hanging on to what I think is important for my life. You know what is important for me far more than I. You know what I truly need. You have a dream for me that is far more than what I could dream. Thank you, Lord, for being with me every step of the way. Thank you for your presence and power, your provision and protection. Thank you, sovereign Lord, for your sovereignty, for in this, I can walk confidently in this life that is ever changing and shifting under my feet (Psalm 46:1–3; Mtt. 7:24–27). Help me see these things and give you glory. Thank you for being my confidence and that I can come before you and rely on you in confidence, confidence in your faithfulness, not mine (Heb. 4:15–16). It is you and you alone that will make all things work out for your good (Rom. 8:28; Phil. 1:6; Ps. 57:2). In your faithfulness, in your character, in your desire for good, I truly can rest and be confident that you have what is best for me in the palm of your righteous right hand. Let me rest in you now, Lord. Help me rest as I give you all my burdens and worries this life of my flesh has wrought on me. Thank you for being my rest and my confidence.

Day Nineteen

The Gift of my Eternal Hope and Perspective—Seeing through My Eyes

&

Therefore we do not lose heart, but though our outer man is decaying, yet our inner man is being renewed day by day. For momentary, light affliction is producing for us an eternal weight of glory far beyond all comparison, while we look not at the things which are seen, but at the things which are not seen; for the things which are seen are temporal, but the things which are not seen are eternal.

2 Cor. 4:16–18

The intent of the original St. Nicholas was to bring hope where there was no hope. He was to provide good feelings of joy and cheer where and when there was little to rejoice and feel good about. He tried to help the otherwise helpless with the soul-warming thought and reality that someone in life truly cared.

In the normal American household, whatever "normal" may mean today, most people likely do not spend too much time thinking about what Christmas truly means. The commercialization and the "Santaization" of Christmas has not just crept in, but overwhelmed and taken over the Christmas scene. On a personal level, this commercialization in the culture certainly has had a negative affect on the heart of man. Getting lost in the hustle and bustle, most I would imagine do not give themselves the time or even want to make the time to really think on the meaning of Christmas.

How easy it is for us to become discouraged, to let the storm clouds of darkness in life fog and blind our thinking and vision of hope. How easy it is to let our frustrations bring us down, to be disappointed and to lose all perspective on what is really important when we are so overwhelmed with our own emotional, strife-filled circumstances, frustrations, and feelings of loneliness. We need a St. Nick, it seems, to come alongside of us to give us hope, to share some joy and optimism, to help bear our burdens. We need someone to help us with a proper perspective and a hopeful view of life when we are so muddled in the quicksand that is the world of flesh, want, greed, and conflict. We need a bright light of hope and a clear vision and perspective to lead the way through the dark storms of life.

℘

"Dear Father, Son and Holy Spirit, blessed Trinity, thank you for making life a joyous possibility. Thank you for making it not just a possibility, but a reality as I turn to you and surrender my all to learn, to rest, and to trust, allowing you to live through me. Thank you that I might live abundantly as you desire, above and through the dark storms that aim to destroy me. Weighed down and blinded in my troubles I lose the proper perspective, Lord. I lose sight of you through the dense and dark fog of my fleshly living. My littleness of faith is shown through my controlling fears. My lack of love is shown through my self-protective pride in selfish independence and shallow relationships, especially with you; my almost non-existent humility and contrition is shown through my false humility; my arrogance and self-serving nature keep me from experiencing your exhilarating life you would have for me, and more importantly, keep you from taking pleasure with me.

"I long for your wonderful light of hope, a hope that is secure and will never desert me even though I walk in a self-made darkness of hopelessness. I long for security and an assurance even though I have planted my heart and my hope in the ways and allurements of the world that are built upon shifting sand (Matthew 7:24). Oh, my Lord, I look at the world that is my life, and I am so caught in the throes of unstable emotions of fear and regret, of anxiety and even paranoia, I sense a noose around my heart strangling out any vital life you have given to me. Forgive me for letting the world of my flesh be so much in control. Forgive me, Lord, for not walking more faithfully, but instead walking by the dictates of my emotional and limited finite perspective. Help me see with your eternal perspective, Lord; help me see through your eyes (Psalm 139:23–24; 2 Corinthians 4:16–5:5). I need this now more than ever. Thank you for your sovereignty and this wonderful gift of being able to see life through your eyes—your sovereign and eternal perspective.

"Help me realize that absolutely everything that happens in my life has gone through you first. You have given it a "check of approval." As you *okayed* Satan to attack Job, so too you have permitted everything in my life. Though it certainly has not been all good from my perspective, it is your sovereignty and your great love and faithfulness in which I can rest, knowing that you are in absolute control and can make all things work out for your good (Rom. 8:28; Ps. 103:19). *For I know that the Lord is great, and that our Lord is above all gods. Whatever the Lord pleases, He does, in heaven and in earth, in the seas and in all deeps* (Ps. 135:5–6). I realize, dear Lord, that I see my problems larger than they really are. I magnify problems and trials rather than magnify you. I fail to see just how infinitely powerful you are. Help me see with your proper perspective. This knowledge of your sovereignty gives me rest, precious rest, for my anxious and fearful soul.

&

Good Christmas morning to you, my hopeful one. This gift of my vision—seeing through my eyes—this gift of my hope, I joyfully give to you this morning and every morning. Please know that my mercies and my loving kindness are new every morning. Please know that each day brings with it a new beginning with new opportunities for us to walk and enjoy life together. Each new day brings with it freedom from your sins and mistakes of yesterday. Each day brings with it new hope for a blessed Christ-like Christmas Day of joy.

My Psalmist, David, says it best when he wrote "Even though I walk through the valley of the shadow of death I will fear no evil." Because why? Because I was with him (Psalm 23). My servant Paul writes that "Even though our outer man is being destroyed, our inner man is being renewed day by day, let us not lose heart." He goes on to say that "This momentary and light affliction" is just that, momentary and light, and it is "producing in us an eternal weight of glory far beyond all comparison." Paul tells you to "not look at the things which are seen, for they are temporal, but to look at the things we are not seen, for they are eternal" (2 Corinthians 4–5). The Spirit writes to you telling you that you are a new creature, old things passed away; "behold", he says, "new things have come (2 Corinthians 5:17)." You can only live in this glorious and freeing truth as you choose to look at your life and this world through my eyes and vision. I would encourage you to not look at the waves or the storm that may surround you; but look to me, for I can calm the storm and still the waves. This I will certainly do in your heart!

I encouraged my disciples to not lose heart but know that I am going to prepare a place for them and that I will come again to receive them to Myself so that where I am they may be also (John 14:1–4). The life you are living now is fleeting; it is but a vapor in the eternal plan of life (Psalm 144:4; 39:4–6). Though "life" seems so large to you now, take heart, as you walk by my side, absolutely nothing is so large of a trial or an obstacle that together we cannot overcome. Remember I am the Creator, the Almighty, the Sovereign of the universe. I am outside of creation yet intimately involved in my creation. In your self-centeredness and the hectic pace of life you have made for yourself, you forget this about me far too often. If you could see just a passing shadow of who I am and my love for you, your worries and fears and insecurities would fade into nothingness (1 John 4:18; Psalm 56).

As it is, you are too involved in trying to control your life from your perspective, with your sense of priorities, principles, and values. You look at the physical and temporal, not at the spiritual and eternal. You look through your eyes of finite flesh in your own strength, and not through the eyes of faith, which are brought to light and life by the infinite wisdom and power of the Holy Spirit. You look too much to that which you can see and understand and control. With this perspective, your problems seem much larger to you than they really are, and I seem much smaller to you than I really am. I persuade you to no longer look at your life this way, but to look to me. If you truly want to gain and live by the security of a solid hope, then get to know me as best as you can. As you try to save your life, you will only end up losing it (Luke 9:24). Live by faith and no longer by sight (1 Corinthians 5:7). If you want a broader and right perspective, close your eyes to the flesh and the world, and let my eyes guide you through your life. Look through my eyes and see the truly big picture of what is really important and what this life is all about. With this perspective your problems that seem so overwhelming will decrease and my power and peace in your life will increase.

You do not have to know answers about yesterday, about today or tomorrow; you do not have to have "it" all planned out; you do not even have to not doubt, for in your weakness of flesh you will always doubt and fail to some degree (Mk. 9:24). Just know me better, and in knowing me better you will see my love for you, my sovereign protection and purpose for you, and my eternal hope and desire for you. In doing this, your faith in living without the need to see and control things, will blossom! Your security and hope in life will not rest on man and this world and especially not on yourself and your limited and finite perspective, but on me, who has your eternal purpose and life in hand (Psalm 16:11; 18:35; 63:8; Isaiah 41:13). You will be deceived by your flesh and by this world for both of these things are temporal and tainted with sin and are corrupt and falling apart. You will never be deceived by me, for I am true and Holy and righteous.

Give me your self-sins of pride, sufficiency, independence, exaltation, which all add up to idolatry; let go of your binding emotions of fear, anxiety, paranoia, and insecurity which these self-sins produce, and let me take over your life (1 Peter 5:6–7). Let me give you the true hope of your life in me, and I in you, and see for the first time from my perspective what this life is really about. It is about me living in you and you living in me (Galatians 2:20). It is about my holiness and my call for you to walk in this holiness (1 Peter 1:15–16). It is about me controlling all things and you controlling nothing (Mark 8:34). It is about me living through you and you dying to the flesh for my sake. It is about me guiding you and you following. It is about me blessing you and taking pleasure in you, as in all you think, say, and do, you bring glory to me (1 Corinthians 10:31; Colossians 3:17).

Merry Christmas, my short-sighted one. May you receive this gift of my eternal sight through my eyes, this eternal perspective of hope, life, truth, and faith for yours and my life together.

༄

"Merry Christmas, Lord, may I only have eyes for you. May the eyes of my heart and mind be on you today, not on my mistakes of yesterday, not on the weaknesses of my flesh or the circumstances of today, and not on the prideful ambition for tomorrow (James 4:13–16). The eternal perspective I so desperately need comes to full vision when I focus on you today, this very moment (Heb. 12:1–2). Help me with this perspective, Lord; help me live each moment as it is–the most important moment of my life spent with you.

I pray this day, this celebration, is honoring to you. I pray to only do this, to honor and glorify you in my heart and with my mouth as I sing songs in my heart of your goodness, holiness, and love. Your sovereign grace, your sovereign holiness, your sovereign goodness, your sovereign love blesses me with assurance that nothing in this world can harm me (Psalm 56; Isaiah 41:10). I am free from worry and fear because of your wondrous sovereignty and love. With this knowledge and this perspective of your sovereignty, I am truly free to enjoy this Christmas season. What a gift you have given me, this gift of being able to see life through your eternal perspective of your sovereignty and love. Thank you once again and always Mighty Savior, Sovereign God.

Day Twenty

the Gift of Time—My New Day for You

❧

This is the day which the Lord has made; let us rejoice and be glad in it.

Ps. 118:24

Therefore be careful how you should walk, not as unwise men, but as wise, making the most of your time, because the days are evil.

Eph. 5:15–16

Christmastime. "It's the most wonderful time of the year", we so gleefully sing. For many, *time* in the season of Christmas goes much too fast and can be over in a blink. For others, the Christmas season drags on and on and on and cannot be over quick enough. The anticipation of Christmas Eve and Christmas morning is almost excruciating to the child at heart. And this Christmastime of the year can be excruciatingly painful in memory of lost ones or in the emotional entanglements of loneliness and despair.

Time; it can be a wonderful Christmas blessing in the traditions we hold on to, and it can also be a fleeting and elusive and a valuable commodity as we waste time in lines, need more time to get "it" all done, and make enough time to spend with family and friends whom we may not have seen in months or years. There is the traditional time set aside for cutting down, putting up, and decorating a Christmas tree. There is the time spent together shopping, and shall we add, not quite an enjoyable time of waiting in lines, being jostled in the hustle and bustle of the myriads of people. And let us never leave out the joyous time spent in mall parking lots just trying to find a parking spot that is not a two-point-six-mile sleigh ride away on which we would not be "making spirits bright" or "laughing all the way."

The question is, *How much of this so precious and valued time do we spend on the One who Christmas is all about?* And, throughout the year do we really appreciate this gift of time we have each day to share life and love with those most important in our lives? This gift of time we have for one another is most important and should take the highest priority in sharing God's love and life with one another.

This new day the Lord has given us should be the most important day of our lives (Psalm 118:24). Yesterday, nor tomorrow, matter. This time we have right now is a time we will never get back so we need to make the most of the time we have in joyous celebration of his life in us (1 Peter 4:2; Ephesians 5:16). Today can be a Christmas day of a new gift of life, a do-over day, a day of freedom from the emotional guilt and hurts of the past and the anxious fears about our tomorrows.

∞

"My Lord, sovereign over all created time and matter, may your creation sing your praises and reflect on the majesty of your splendor and holiness this fine day. I must first confess and ask you to forgive me for the lack of time I spend with you. I move on in my life as if living this horizontal life is the most important thing I can do. I make up a list of things I need to do today, people I am to meet, places I need to be, all the while I neglect spending time with you. I was about to say, I neglect fitting you into my agenda. How shameful this is. I should not put you on my agenda; you are my agenda. Nor do I want to go someplace or do something and ask you to come along, as if on a leash. What foolish and naïve arrogance. Lord, I want you to lead, to guide, and direct. I want you to be my destination; then you can take me where you want to go. I thank you, Lord, for desiring and allowing me to come along with you today. I know to do this, Lord, I need to spend more time with you. I need to spend all my time with you. I need to give back to you my life and time you have first given me. I need you to help me with this, Lord. Guide me, I pray."

ᘓ

My busy child, yes you do go at a hectic pace of life, going nowhere fast at times. You are kind of like a little hamster that runs in a wheel inside its cage. It is putting out a lot of energy and is using up a lot of time, but going nowhere. But I have not made you to be like a hamster spinning in your wheel of self importance and self-ambition going no where. I have made you and have called you out of this "hamster-like cage of life" and have given you something much more valuable to do with your day and time. That is primarily spending your day–your time, to be with me!

Let me ask you a question, dear one. What is so important in your life that you sacrifice and neglect spending time with me? You say you have important things to do, you have a schedule to maintain and places to be and people to meet, and, and, and. And then when you think you have gotten it all done, you find that it is not all done. You find more to do; thus, you rarely have time for me or your family and friends with whom I have blessed your life. Who put you on this running wheel, and why is it so important for you to do this to yourself? Why have you taken this precious gift of time I have given you today, this time to enjoy and grow in your relationships, this time to learn of me, this time to come along with me, to work with me, and use this time for your own selfish supposed needs of performance and accomplishments and self-improvement?

Though this may sound like somewhat of a paradox, if you want to spend more time with family and friends, which is what I want you to do, then you must spend more time with me. The truth is, in not spending time with me and giving me your best, you will only run out of time and energy for the things you think are so important. You will sacrifice true peace and joy and vitality for your life by not making me the "time of your life."

෮

Your time on this earth is short. It is valuable. It is precious in my sight. I wish you would see it this way. The devil would want to rob you of this time with me (John 10:10), by convincing you to use the time you have to busy yourself in making your own life work (Genesis 3:4–5). The world's priorities of making money, making a living so you can buy things and more things to occupy more of your time, steals your time so in the end neither I nor your family or friends have any of your time. The devil would also like to rob you of your time by leading you to live in regret or guilt or in a nonforgiving mode of living. He would like nothing better than for you to waste your day ruminating on your past mistakes, hurts, and the "unfairness of life," and thus do nothing about them, except, be controlled by them.

My child, I need to tell you the radical priority I

would have for you in understanding the big picture, then a few insights for using this gift of time most wisely. I do not want you to "make time" for me by cutting something out of your daily living. Forget the ten, fifteen, or even thirty minutes in the morning, at lunch, or on the treadmill at the health club, or, as you fall asleep. Is that all I am worth to you? I do not want to just be "fit in" to your schedule as you might fit in some time for a friend or business partner for lunch on Thursday. I do not want to be scheduled "in" your life— kind of like tagging along with all those things you have to do. I want to be your life! I do not want some of your time, I want all of your time. This is the radical priority and perspective you need to see and have. I know this may sound possessive or controlling. Let me just tell you that I desire a wonderful and full and abundant life for you, and in order to accomplish this for you, I need your all (Psalm 37:1–6).

Realize you cannot control time; though try as you might to do this. The more you try to control the time you have, the more time will control you. You will never have enough time, or time will go by just too slow. You will never be content with this. Being impatient, stressing, and getting angry over being late, worrying about not having enough time, or too much idle (and idol) time, is not a very comfortable prison in which to put yourself.

Surrender to me your time including all you plans, your relationships, your career, and dreams and as you allow me to, I will bless you with the right priorities and blessings in life that are far beyond what you can imagine (John 10:10; Eph. 1:3; Proverbs 3:13–17; 8:10–11). You will be content because your life will be rested on my time for you and no longer dependent on your time you try to make for yourself (Matt. 6:24; 1Tim. 6:6; Ps. 37:4).

Prayerfully give me all the "time in your life" so I can then give back to you the "time of your life." Do not be afraid to give me your all in this way. The time I give you right now, which is the most important time of your life, will come alive when you do this.

My gift of time for you is not about reclaiming time lost yesterday or worrying about time in the future; it is about the wondrous experience of my presence in your life now—this new day! Can being anxious or consumed with the past add anything to your life (Matthew 6:27)? No, it cannot. It can only rob you of the joy of this moment—time spent with me!

My gift of time for you is not about living selfishly, but it is about living selflessly in your relationships, as I live for you (John 13:15, 34; Philippians 2:3–4). Do not hold on to a grudge or withhold forgiveness. Do not give the devil an opportunity to steal this day away from you in this way (Ephesians 4:27). Today is the day of working out your salvation (Philippians 3:12–13), and a day to "let all bitterness and wrath and anger and clamor and slander be put away from you, along with all malice. And be kind to one another, tender-hearted, forgiving each other, just as God in Christ also has forgiven you" (Ephesians 4:31–32). What huge emotional and spiritual freedom there is in doing this.

Merry Christmas, my time-bound child. May each day, each moment be an eternal Christmas moment of celebration of this gift for you. A moment of time spent with me is greater than a life time with the best this world has to offer (Psalm 63:3). Spending your time with me would certainly make this "The most wonderful time and day of the year!"

℘

"Thank you, Lord, for this awareness of how precious time is, especially time with you, which should be, always. Thank you for this gift of time that is so obvious that I simply take full advantage of it in living for self all the while not giving you praise or thanks for it. I realize I have spent too much time with my priorities in this world. As your word convicts me, time is short, the last days are upon us, therefore I must *conduct myself in holiness and godliness* (2Pet. 3:11). Forgive me for letting the world steal so much of this precious gift of time that should be spent with you. Today is the most important time in my life. Help me make it the most important and most exhilarating time of my life in living for you. I give you all my life and time so you can accomplish what you will through me and for me. Thank you for this Christmastime. May this be truly *a most wonderful time of the year* (day) for you and me."

Day Twenty-one

the Gift of My Friendship with You—the Gift of Relationships

&

You are my friends if you do what I command you. No longer do I call you slaves, for the slave does not know what his master is doing; but I have called you friends, for all things that I have heard from My Father I have made know to you.

John 15:14–15

By this all men will know that you are My disciples, if you have love for one another.

John 13:35

L et's see, we have Mr. Claus and Mrs. Claus. There is of course the special and most charming connection between Santa and his elves and reindeer of the North Pole. Let us not forget Mr. Ebenezer Scrooge and Bob Cratchet, or the Grinch and those in "Whoville". Joseph and Mary had the providential hand upon theirs as the angels in heaven were curiously watching from above. The most profound is the "oneness" of the Father, Son and Holy Spirit. Close behind this is the most important as far as you are concerned, it is the Babe in the manger–Jesus, and you! What are we talking about? We are talking about relationships.

What is one of your fondest Christmas memories? I bet it involved a family member or a friend. When you think about giving gifts, you of course think of whom you are going to be buying for and giving to. Someone at the Christmas dinner table has to pass you the mashed potatoes, or the turkey, or the stuffing, or the goose leg or figgy pudding. Of course you get the proverbial and annual fruitcake from Aunt Wilma or Uncle Fred or that office partner who may or may not like you very much. When you are telling family stories that make you either laugh or cry, you are talking with another about another in your life. When you are singing those wonderful Christmas songs it is either you or Grandpa Jack or Auntie Laur-Laur that is off key, making the melody and the day bright, right?

Christmas is about relationships. And, so is life—life with Jesus first, then life with others (Matthew 22:36–39; 10:37–39). He has come to this earth to don the flesh so we could enter into the most mysterious and profound and yet the most intimate relationship with him. His gift of life to us is about his gift of relationship with us. And this personal gift is a model for the gift of relationships we are to have with one another: *Therefore be imitators of God, as beloved children; and walk in love just as Christ also loved you…* (Eph. 5:1–2). I dare say, we do not live in our relationships with this example and his gift of love, mercy, grace, and humility nearly enough, if at all.

Living this life is incomplete without relationships. In fact it is not just incomplete, it is empty, desolate, and desperate. Only in relationships can we grow and learn in love, compassion, and empathy. Only in relationships can we learn to trust, be vulnerable and humble, and learn a needed dependence upon another (1Cor. 12:7, 25). Only in relationships can we learn to be more like Jesus as we give up our own interests, give up our own lives for the building up of another. Only in relationships can we be Jesus to another. God made us for relationships. We cannot make it alone. God did not make us to be *pridefully* independent of one another but to be dependent in love with one another (Genesis 2:18, 23–25; 1Cor. 12:7, 12–25; John 17:21–22). Adam was not complete until there was Eve, and neither are we complete until we have Jesus, and, one another.

Why did Jesus come? So we might enter into a relationship with him, so our relationship with the Father might be made new (Ephesians 2:1–8; John 1:12; 2 Corinthians 5:17). He came so we might understand what relationships are all about as we look at the loving, humble, selfless, and unifying relationship within the Trinity! Then, as we continue to learn and grow from this, we use this knowledge of love, humility, and selflessness in our relationships with another. Jesus, in praying to the Father, asked to make his disciples "one," *even as we are one* (John 17:11). This oneness is strange to us today. It is too hard, too risky, too frightening in this day and age of looking out for "number one", in this current cultural philosophy of "me-ism" to be so openly vulnerable and humble and God-honoring in our relationships.

৪৩

"My wonderful friend, Jesus, my trusted heavenly ally, my compatriot so faithful to me. As you are to me may I be the same to you, faithful and true. Thank you for being so for me. Thank you, my gracious Savior, for renewing and establishing a personal and reconciliatory relationship with me. My generous and limitless King, thank you ever so much for my family and friends. I pray, Lord, that you help me become a friend to them as you are to me. I pray that I could so empty myself of self so that it is you living through me that is a friend to them."

"Lord, relationships are so dear to you, and I fear I more often than not abuse and take advantage, I manipulate and use, I so neglect the relationships you have put in my life. This starts with my relationship with you. I do these things to your disappointment and sorrow, and my frustration and hurt. Help me see the needful purpose of your design and desire for relationships in my life. Help me see, Lord, that as I do to another, I do as unto you (Matt. 25:34–40). Help me Lord truly appreciate each and every person you have brought into my life, for it is with these precious people, even the ones I may not particularly like, I can become more like you as I humble myself in following your example of your love and forgiveness in your relationship with me (Eph. 4:1–3, 5:1–2).

ಬ

My chosen friend, chosen to be in relationship with me, Merry Christmas to you this day. I have made you for relationships, first with me, then as you allow me to live through you, with your world of family and friends and with neighbors and strangers you do not yet know. I am all about relationships.

Did you know that I desire to spend every day, even every moment with you? Do not pass this truth over lightly. Hear it again: I desire to spend every day, even every moment with you. Did you know that I rejoice when you rejoice, and I cry when you cry? Do you realize I have a hope and a dream for you that are truly wonderful and exciting? Do you realize that if you were the only person to save on this planet I would still go to the cross for you? Why? Simply because I love you. Simply because I long to have and grow in a relationship with you.

This Christmas season, which should be every day of the year, let me encourage you to see me in every relationship in your life. It could be the relationship you have with your employer or employee, your teacher or mentor, your neighbor, friend, certainly with your family members, and yes, even your dentist and your mother-in-law (Ephesians 5:21; Romans 12–13).

Appreciate these relationships. I can do great things in them. Give thanks for your relationships and continually work on your relationships, for this blesses and honors me. Honor your relationships by following my way of putting the other's interests before your own, and perhaps most importantly, forgiving one another as I have forgiven you (Philippians 2:3; John 13:15; Eph. 4:32). In doing this I will be glorified, and your relationship and your life will flourish and be blessed in my presence.

❧

I am presently not with you physically, so our relationship might seem a little distant, if not strained at times (Psalm 13). This makes life harder for you and more difficult to understand. But know this: I am absolutely with you in the person and in the power of the Holy Spirit. You may not feel his presence all the time, but know the truth that he is with you forevermore. I am also with you through the lives of other people. If they know me or even if they do not know me, I can use them to help guide you, encourage you, convict you, comfort you, and love you. Through them I can teach you the virtue of patience and the most awesome godly quality of forgiveness. Your friend has a view of your life you do not have. I may use that friend to help you see this needed view. I can give them wisdom to counsel you and show you things that you would not otherwise see. That person in relationship with you has strengths that I can use to build you up when you are weak, and in their weaknesses, you can help them overcome with your strengths, as I live through you.

The gift of relationship is truly one of my favorite gifts. There is no more exciting and vital way through which I can do great things in your life and the life of others. Please understand your relationships on earth will never be as they can and should be unless you are in a vulnerable and trusting relationship with me. In your fleshly relationships you have a weakness to look for love, value, acceptance, and purpose before you look for these things in me. This will lead your relationships down a rocky path of stress, frustration and even strife.

One of the greatest and most vital ways for you to grow in me and in your relationships is that of forgiveness. Never are you more like me when you forgive. In the strength and in obedience of the Spirit go to another and extend forgiveness when they have wronged you, and ask for forgiveness when you have wronged them (Matt. 5:23–24). Give it and grant it unconditionally. Choose to not remember or bring up any hurt your friend has caused you; hold it not against them. As I have forgiven you of your sins that kept us eternally estranged, and as I forgive you as you come to me daily (Matt. 6:12; 1John 1:9), do the same in your relationships. Free yourself from the chains and prison walls bitterness, of holding a grudge and the hurt and even anger you may be feeling. As I have given you the *gift* of forgiveness, give this gift to one another.

My disciples said, *Lord, increase our faith,* as I was instructing them about forgiveness (Luke 17:1–10). Forgiveness is a divine quality requiring divine strength, and it is only as you surrender your life to me that you can truly forgive. I encourage you to look only to me for all your needs, and then together, we can be a blessing in all your relationships. Though there may be great fear in trusting another, in being vulnerable and loving and ready to forgive another, there is tremendous blessing and reward in laying your life so open in your relationships (Psalm 133:1). Holding on to self in pride, protecting yourself in fear of being controlled, used, or even hurt will only hinder if not eventually destroy relationships I desire for you (Ephesians 4:25–29; James 4:1–2). You will also be giving the Devil a foothold, an opportunity to control your life and destroy your witness of my grace and love in you in this world (Eph. 5:25–32; Matt. 5:13–16).

Look at my life and see that I entrusted all my relationships to the Father. My value, acceptance, love and purpose did not come from or was satisfied by man, my closest disciples, even myself. These things came from my Father. I did not first trust man, but first trusted my Father. In this way I was used for his purposes for his glory. In doing this I could have an open and vulnerable relationship with others not fearing what man could do to me (Psalm 56). Even though I knew my friends and disciples would desert me, I did not fear this or let it limit my love and compassion for them. My relationships were selfless, not full of self.

Look to me for your love first and foremost (1 John 4;19; Rev. 2:4), and then take that bold step of faith, trust me, and go and love others selflessly and sacrificially, holding on to nothing of your own life. Love as I have loved you (John 13:14; Eph. 5:1–2). I entrusted my life to the Father, so you too, entrust your life and your relationship to the Father. I know you will get hurt in relationships; that is the way it is for this life in the flesh, but let me take care of that for you. You just be me to them.

I have made you as a relational being. This is part of what it means to be created in my image. To have a wonderful and liberating and loving relationship with me, and together with me have a special relationship with another is a Christmas gift I always want you to treasure. It is a very special gift, requiring special care, and I hope you can simply and innocently rejoice and revel in each and every relationship I bless you with. I am never more alive in you then when you trust me by not putting up walls of self-protection motivated by a self-love and a prideful fear in your relationships. Let me shine through your life for others to see and embrace. In doing this I bring this gift of each relationship to life for a heavenly Christmas blessing from me to you to others. As I am a Christmas gift to you, you be a Christmas gift to another.

&C

"Thank you, dearest Friend. Thank you for letting me call you friend. Lord, I pray that I might first and foremost love you and honor you and embrace you in the relationship you have established with me. May this be cherished beyond all else. May you be honored in all my relationships today, Lord, may you be honored. Help me not live selfishly with others, but live selflessly for others so you can be glorified and your will be done in my relationships. Help me honor those you have brought into my life. Thank you for this gift. May I give back to you all my relationships and ask you to bless them that you might be glorified. Humble me, Lord, to receive this gift of relationships, this gift love in honor of you."

Day Twenty-two

the Gift of my Protection—the Armor of God

&

Finally, be strong in the Lord, and in the strength of His might. Put on the full armor of God, that you may be able to stand firm against the schemes of the devil.

Eph. 6:10–11

Okay, tell the truth. How many of you at whatever age have scurried and rummaged through the presents under the tree, giving them a shake or two, checking out their size, weight, shape, and sound? Did you know there is what is called the "shrakeable" factor for those with true Christmas present-discerning-gift passion? The "shrakeable" factor is tactilely and audibly discerned with ultra-sensitive (special tactile) sensor chips embedded in the fingertips to discern how much the present rattles and bounces around in the box when you shake it? Hence, the "shrakeable" factor. As you do this, you only hope this present is not breakable; otherwise, you would have to answer to Mrs. Claus. And she most likely would not be treating you to some hot chocolate and chocolate chip cookies fresh from her oven if you broke one of her husband's presents.

Isn't it kind of fun to get those somewhat different-shaped packages; you know, anything that is not a "clothes box" that has some rattling and rolling to them? Maybe it is a guy thing, I don't know, but isn't it fun to get toys or something you can play with and put together, of course without reading the directions or instruction manual (as my wife likes to do)?

Well, this gift we can certainly shake, and when we shake it we hear and feel a lot of rattling and rolling around in the box. The good news about this present is, and you can tell this to Mrs. Claus, that this gift is impossible to break—it is of supernatural/heavenly origin (though you do not know this yet)! There is certainly some hands-on play factor we have here. There are many shapes and weights in this box to keep you interested and involved for a lifetime, and not just shaking the package under the tree on Christmas morning. You can see through the wrapping, as you pretend not to look, there are some very interesting pictures on the box. You see a belt of some sort that has a buckle on it with what seems to be lightning bolts charging from it. You see some shoes—really cool ones—looks like all-terrain shoes with lots of hooks and laces. It even has a compass built in to the toe of the shoe (cooool!). You can slightly make out what looks like some armor-looking breastplate that glows in the dark and a shield with many lines of texture and decorations on them. There is a picture of a helmet unlike any helmet you have seen, and what you think to be something like … yes, it is a sword with glistening sharp edges that has a luminous, greenish glow around it.

This gift seems to be really cool—the real "gift-getting" deal! Once you open it, you see that this gift requires some assembly, and you will need an energy source—not of this world by the way—which makes this gift "way cool." You have all the tools you need, but there is supervision that is required that you are uncertain about obeying (naturally so—this is your gift and you want to be in charge, right?). Right on the front of the box you read: "Armor of God: the Most Powerful Armament in the Universe!" And in slightly smaller letters in a bright gold color you read: 'Cannot be used alone. The instruction manual must be kept with you at all times to be read before using and periodically through its lifetime of use." As fun and important and cool as all this stuff is, without the instruction manual and required supervision, this gift, though it cannot break, could be rendered useless. That is, it can be disappointing, frustrating and, *unfun*— by way of ignorance, arrogance, and presumption!

છ

"Dear Lord, my Mighty King and Warrior, thank you for this gift of your armor. Only you know the battles that lay before me and are building up inside of me. Only you know the enemy terrain into which I travel, for you have been there and have come forth victoriously. I must confess, Lord, that I so often feel defeated and stuck behind enemy lines, held captive by bounds of doubt, fear, error, and littleness of faith, not to mention my pride and self-centeredness that only accentuates all these weaknesses of self. May you be pleased to save me yet again today, Lord. Be pleased to save me for your namesake (Psalm 18:19).

"The battle rages around and within my life (2 Corinthians 1:6–10; 7:5; Romans 8:5–8; Ephesians 6:12). Help me, Lord. Help me do battle, to stand firm, and to not give in and surrender myself to the enemy in this world and even my own thoughts, emotions and fleshy impulses. Help me stand firm in you to give you my all so you may be your all in and through me. Help me, Lord, win my battles, not for my glory but for yours. Help me, Lord, not give the enemy any bragging rights over me, but let him turn, run, and hide as it is you to glorify yourself through me (James 4:7; Ps. 31:14–17). Thank you for this gift of your armor. Help me don this armor and wear this in a worthy manner. Thank you for guiding me and protecting me wherever you would have me go, to walk humbly and confidently in this world glorifying you, my Commander and Chief, my Savior and Redeemer.

છ

Listen to my words, my young Christmas warrior, "For who is God, but the Lord? And who is a Rock, except our God, the God who girds me with strength, and makes my way blameless? He makes my feet like hinds' feet, and sets me upon my high places. He trains my hands for battle, so that my arms can bend a bow of bronze. Thou hast given me the shield of Thy salvation, and Thy right hand upholds me; and Thy gentleness makes me great. Thou dost enlarge my steps under me, and my feet have not slipped" (Psalm 18:31–36). "The Lord is my light and my salvation; whom shall I fear? The Lord is the defense of my life; whom shall I dread? When evildoers came upon me to devour my flesh, my adversaries and my enemies, they stumbled and fell. Though a host encamp against me, my heart will not fear; though war arise against me, in spite of this I shall be confident … for in the day of trouble he will conceal me in his tabernacle; in the secret place of his tent he will hide me; he will life me up on a rock … Wait for the Lord; be strong and let your heart take courage; yes, wait for the Lord" (Psalm 27: 1–3, 5–6, 14).

ॐ

Stand firm, mighty warrior, and know this battle you face is not a battle against flesh and blood but against rulers, against the powers, against the world forces of this darkness, against the spiritual forces of wickedness in the heavenly places (Ephesians 6:12). Stand firm and know that this battle is mine (Ephesians 6:10, 14; 2 Chronicles 20:15; 32:8; Zechariah 4:6). Stand firm; for I have come to destroy the works and schemes of the Devil (Heb. 2:14; 1John 3:8).

Stand firm my child and take this belt of truth (Ephesians 6:14; John 17:17) and wrap it around your waist. Pull in all that loose clothing—those things that are made of erroneous thinking, untruths, and lies that make you stumble in doubt. The enemy will surely grab these untruths and lies and deceptions that you wear and throw you about mercilessly. Gird yourself with only truth from me and about me (Romans 13:14). I am your greatest truth (John 14:6). Know me and my words, especially concerning your identity, and the enemy can grab hold of nothing (John 8:32). The enemy will tell you sweet-sounding lies about yourself to puff you up on one hand, and on the other, he will try to convince you that you are no good, unworthy, useless, a loser, too stupid, ugly, and unacceptable. He will attack you where you are weakest. It may be your pride or your false humility (really the same thing). It may be your greed or lust, envy, or jealousy. It will be what you lust for and try to control. He will try to use the wisdom of the world to lure you away (Genesis 3:1–5; Matthew 4:1–11; 2 Corinthians 11:14–15) from me—your living truth. He will confuse you with temptations to be the god of your own life (Gen. 3:5). Do not listen to him, but cinch up this gift of the belt of truth and do not believe his lies (John 8:44; 2 Corinthians 11:3, 14–15). Believe the truth and trust only me.

Put on my breastplate of righteousness (Romans 13:14; 2 Corinthians 5:21). To do this, you must first take off your own effort of self-righteousness. There is nothing you can do in your own righteousness that can please me, or that which you can use in your battles in life (Hebrews 11:6; Romans 3:10; Ephesians 6:12). In fact, as you hold on to your own sense of righteousness, the enemy will surely use this against you. It is your pride which he can use as the greatest weapon against you (Proverbs 16:18). Give this up to me now, and never try to take it back. It is a most vile weapon of the enemy to which you are so vulnerable. Your flesh, your own sense of righteousness, will profit you nothing (John

15:5; 6:63), it will only weaken you and give the enemy a hold over your life (Genesis 3:15; 4:7; Proverbs 16:18). As you surrender this prideful life to me, put on my life (Romans 13:14), put on my righteousness (2 Corinthians 5:21). Accept it as a gift; think not it is anything you have to work for. The enemy will try to convince you otherwise. He will try to tell you that you had to earn this gift of my righteousness and because you can earn it, so you can lose it. This is not true. Only in me are you righteous and only in me can you stand firm to this lie and deception and attack of the enemy.

Now, put on these shoes of the gospel of peace (Ephesians 6: 15). Take these shoes and fulfill your purpose for which I have called you. I have called you in peace by making peace between you and my Father—between you and your Father in heaven. You will walk in this world full of strife and conflict; it is full of hatred and violence. But with these shoes of peace, you will be my messenger. As you humbly walk in my wisdom and my ways (Ephesians 4:1–3; 5:1–21), though you will be attacked (1 Peter 4:12–13), you will be walking in my shoes and my ways, and no enemy can thwart my purpose or destiny for you (Psalm 56:3–6, 9–11). Though you will walk on the slippery slopes of temptation and sin, though you may walk in the blinding light of falseness and deceptive lies (2 Corinthians 11:3, 14–15), walk in confidence in me, and these shoes will protect you and will guide you safely through any and all enemy terrain (Psalm 18:36; 23:4–5; 27:1–3).

The enemy will not hold back his missiles of doubt, fear, confusion, and man's wisdom of trusting in only himself. Raise this gift of the shield of faith (Ephesians 6:16; Psalm 18:2, 28:7, 91:4). Let this shield protect you from his flaming missiles attacking your prideful flesh, weak emotions, and independent and self-centered thinking. Do not put faith in yourself; do not trust yourself for your fleshly controlled heart is not always on our side (Jeremiah 17:9; Romans 7:5; 8:5–8). You can try to muster up enough faith to walk, to stand firm to fight the battle, but in your own faith by your own strength, you will often, if not always, fail. In using this piece of armor, please know it is not the size of your faith that makes this armor work, it is your little bit of faith planted in my great faith and power that will rescue and provide for you (Matthew 17:20). Trust in me and trust not in yourself. Surrender to me and allow me to live and battle through you. I will hold up this shield as you look to me to do so. For I am your shield (Psalm 18:2; 28:7; 91:4)

Put on this helmet of salvation (Ephesians 6:17), my child, you desperately need this. Rest assured that you are mine and that your salvation is of no work of your own (Ephesians 2:8–9). The instruction manual tells you that I have saved you because I delight in you (Psalm 18:19). The wonderful meaning of this salvation is that I now live in you (Galatians 2:20; Colossians 1:27–28). Because I am in you, and you are in me, we can walk through this life with assurance that nothing will nor can overwhelm you. Your salvation is your new identity, your new purpose, your new power, definition, and direction in life (2 Corinthians 5:17–21). The enemy will do all he can to take this assurance away from you. He will try to destroy you as he did Eve in the garden by enticing her to doubt my words and promises. Don't let him do this to you. Stand firm in the truth of who you are in me and let my choosing you—your salvation, be a stronghold that the enemy can in no way penetrate.

A final piece of armament is what I used when tempted, it is the Word of God—the sword of the spirit (Matthew 4:1–11). It will slice, dash, and chop up any temptations and untruths the world and the enemy can throw at you. Be aggressive with this armor. *It is writ-*

ten, were the words I used when I was tempted. You use them as well. Let my words richly dwell in your heart (Colossians 3:16). Fill your mind with what is truth, stay focused on me (Hebrews 12:2)—the living Word, the living truth, and take captive all those tempting and errant thoughts by holding them captive to my Word of truth (2 Corinthians 10:5). The enemy will use subtle and sweet-sounding lies and half-truths to creep inside your armament (2 Corinthians 11:14–15). Do not let this happen. As you see him approaching, use my words in your heart and mind and stand firm to his deceptions and lies.

There is one last thing I must tell you. To most effectively put on this armor and use this armor, we must do it together! And to do it together, you must pray. Pray at all times, with all perseverance and petition (1Thess. 5:17). Pray for yourself, pray for others, and pray for my will to be done. Never give up prayer. Prayerfully put this armor on each and every day. It is imperative. There is no power in the armor without prayer. In prayer you allow me to bring to life the full power of this armor; you invite me to do battle for you (1 Samuel 17:47; 2 Chronicles 20:15).

Merry Christmas, my "Christmas warrior." Though that may sound a bit contradictory, it is not. The enemy would like to destroy the meaning of Christmas in your life and in the world. Don this armor as my gift to you, and walk in celebration of my Christmas message wherever you go, spreading cheer of the good news to the world so needy.

೮೦

"Thank you, Lord, for so much great "stuff." Thank you for thinking of everything. Thank you for giving me everything I need to live a life of godliness and in victory for you! Thank you, gracious Savior, that not only have you given me this armor, but as I surrender to you, you will help me use it. It is your life that makes this work. May I always look to you as I don this armor for your glory and honor. Thank you so much for this necessary gift of life."

Day Twenty-three

the Gift of Prayer and My Prayer for You

છ

Be anxious for nothing, but in everything by prayer and supplication with thanksgiving let your requests be made known to God. And the Peace of God, which surpasses all comprehension, shall guard your hearts and your minds in Christ Jesus.

Phil. 4:6–7

In my distress, I called upon the Lord, and cried to my God for help; He heard my voice out of His temple, and my cry for help before Him came into His ears.

Ps. 18:6

Remember writing to Santa, or even talking to Santa concerning things in your life that were most important—like your Christmas list? In the Charlie Brown Christmas cartoon, Sally, Charlie's sister, was putting together a letter and list to Santa. In her letter she said she had been especially good through the year, and because of this she was requesting, ever so politely and sweetly of course, a just reward for her good behavior. In her letter she was specifying to Santa about the shape, size, color, and quantity of each present, and if that was too much of an inconvenience, she told Santa it would be okay if he just sent tens and twenties. Charlie Brown, after reading this list, throws her letter in the air and walks away in disgust that even this *Christmas greed monster thing* had gotten to his sister. "Doesn't anybody know what Christmas is all about?" he would ask at least a couple of times in the story. Sally, so undaunted by her brother's reaction, calmly says that she simply deserves what should be coming to her. All she wants and deserves is her "fair share." I wonder do we ever take this attitude about life as if "life" owes us something, even to God?

So, what is on your Christmas wish list? Real estate, tens and twenties, your "fair share?" I remember on my list I would have expensive items on the top of the list and the least expensive items on the bottom (I hope I was not alone in this). "Well, if you cannot get me this, then you can get me that. And if you cannot get me that, then … (and on down the list went, decreasing in value). I wonder if we do not secretly put together a list and hope to get some cool stuff (from God?). And how about when your list is out there, you know, among family and friends, do you feel expectant, thinking, *Oh boy, I am going to rake in the Christmas bounty this year!*

Let us go from Sally and Santa to you and the Savior. Here is a question for you: What is it we would ask for if God were to ask us for such a list, and it was he doing the supplying of our requests? Now that should get us thinking. Would it be as materialistic as a new car, a new home, money, or other fun wants in life that would be for the most part purely a luxury, that is, not a necessity? Or, would it be for a change in circumstances, a new job perhaps, financial security, healing, or benefit for others or self? How about "genie-type' requests, like the want to have great riches or power and control, to be better looking, to be smarter or to be more likeable? I think we could break down any request list into three categories: would your list be more self-centered, other-centered, or God-centered?

Do you know what Solomon's prayer request was when God was doing the asking? It was God-centered for the sake of God in serving his people. It was for wisdom to do his best in living for his God. It was not for riches, wealth, personal honor, or glory etc. (2 Chronicles 1:8–12). It was for the glory of God.

Jesus, in his prayer in the garden before he went to the cross, prayed that through his life the Father would be glorified (John 17:1). A common prayer theme weaved throughout the whole book of Scripture is for God to be exalted and glorified with grateful and humble hearts.

Prayer is not a wish list as a Christmas list might be considered. Often though, we treat our prayer needs as if they were on a Christmas list of sorts. Prayer is a gift from God that is so often neglected by some, abused by others, and most often not appreciated or understood by most. Prayer is about holy and reverent communion with the Creator and Sustainer God of the universe. We cannot let this realization of who we are communing with pass us by. We think so little of this, and even less, let this fact affect our lives. Think of how easy it is for us to be in awe over seeing and meeting a famous celebrity. It seems we can be so awed over another human, but when it comes to meeting God in prayer; well, that is certainly not as exciting or "awe-inspiring" as say, meeting a top Hollywood actor, rock star, or a sports hero. And we wonder why our prayer and spiritual life, and our life in general, may seem rather flat, shall we say.

Prayer is not for the purpose of primarily hanging a laundry (or Christmas) list of wants in the face of God. Though God wants to hear from us, the truth is, he knows what is on our "laundry list" before we do (Matthew 6:8; Psalm 139:4; Isaiah 65:24). Prayer is not for him to learn "stuff" about us, but it is for us to learn and experience, him. Prayer is not so much for us to request a change in our circumstances, but prayer enables him to change us. This change happens as we invite him into our daily lives through prayer. This changes our perspective, priorities, attitudes, emotions, and ways of living; through increased and continual prayer, it will be Jesus living more vitally through us and for us.

Prayer is a most cherished gift we should never neglect or not appreciate, and as the commercial states about the American Express credit card, "We should never leave home without it." I think we can safely say, "If we live life without prayer, we essentially live life without God."

℘

"Oh Merciful Savior, I come before you with a bowed heart to thank you for prayer. Thank you for your graciousness and loving patience to hear the same prayers from me for perhaps the hundredth time. Thank you for understanding my weakness and insecurities. May you, Lord, once again be open to my prayer; and in fact, dear Spirit, please pray for me (Romans 8:26). I cannot trust my heart to pray for myself, for I fear my greedy and self-centered heart would not honor your gift and privilege of prayer. I am afraid, Lord, I would only make my prayer out to be just a Christmas-type list of what I want, not necessarily what I truly need, and most importantly not what you want for me. You know my weakness and my needs far better than I. I am too emotionally bound to my own suffering and want of comfort to truly know to pray in your will.

"Pray for me, Lord, and as you do, I wait to hear what you have to say to me. Lord I pray not wanting anything from you; I just want you. Make me know thy ways, oh Lord; teach me thy paths. Lead me in thy truth and teach me. For thou art the God of my salvation; for thee I wait all the day (Psalm 25:4–6). In thee, oh Lord, I have taken refuge; let me never be ashamed; in thy righteousness deliver me quickly; be thou to me a rock of strength, a stronghold to save me. For thou are my rock and my fortress; for thy namesake thou will lead me and guide me (Psalm 31:1–3).

ಜ

I love hearing from you, my child. And I truly appreciate it when you listen to me (Matthew 6:7). What you have to tell me in your prayer is not surprising to me. I know what your prayers are even before you pray it (Isaiah 65:24). What is really wonderful in your praying is that you are giving me freedom to enter into your life through this personal and prayerful communion with you. Listen as you come in prayer, listen that you may hear, that your eyes and ears would be open to my wisdom and truth (Ephesians 1:18–19; 2:14–20; Isaiah 55:3). Listen that you may live fully. Listen that I would guide you in my will. Listen that you may be refreshed by my gentle whisperings of truth, encouragement, and even conviction. For my word to you in prayer restores your soul; it rejoices your heart; it enlightens your eyes (Psalm 19:7–11).

I want you to pray unceasingly (1 Thessalonians 5:17). I want you to always have me in the center of your focus as you journey through life, moment by moment. I encourage you to do this not for my sake, but for yours. In doing this, there is great life and strength and hope. In doing this, you increasingly get to know me. Through prayer my peace will begin to overwhelm you (Philippians 4:6–7). As you pray you increase in seeing through my eyes with my eternal perspective. The more you humbly pray the more the security of my sovereign control will reign in your heart. The more you humbly pray the more my life will become vitally alive and real to you. Experiencing my presence in prayer brings eternal hope and heavenly riches where there was once temporal hopelessness and fleshly depravity; it provides sure direction where there was once aimlessness. It builds enduring strength where there was once failing weakness, and enhances and revitalizes a vibrant life where there was once a lingering death.

Prayer will change circumstances at times if it is my will to do so. But prayer will always change you if you allow me to do this work in you. Prayer is not so my will can come alongside of your will, granting those things you think you want and need. Prayer is your will surrendering to my will gifting you with those things I know to be best in and for your life.

I am your best friend, and I want you to be mine. In order for this to happen, we need to spend time together, lots of time, all of time, now and eternally. If in your most trusting, joyous, and intimate relationship with a friend, there comes a conflict of some sort, what do you do? You talk to that person. You work out that conflict. The result is you understand that person better. Your relationship grows even stronger. Well, this is what I want for us. I want our relationship to grow ever closer so you will you will know what I am thinking, what I would do, and what I am feeling. This is my life come alive in you. This only can happen through prayer. I am intimately involved in your life. Together "we will" live life! Do you not just love that, *we will* live life *together!* I pray you see my heart's desire this way.

Merry Christmas, my prayer child and my prayer partner. You are my prayer partner, for I need you to pray for my saints who are in this world (Ephesians 6:18), and I need you to pray for my will to be done (Matt. 6:10). May you receive my gift of prayer, and, my prayer and desire for you this Christmastime. And oh yeah, if you are wondering what it is on my Christmas list, what I would like from you? Well, that is easy. I want you. That's all. As you give me you, guess what? Your prayer list comes along with you, and as this is surrendered to me, then I will do great things in giving you the desires of my heart on your heart (Psalm 37:4, 145:14–16; Matthew 6:33).

✺

"My Generous Savior, may I always look to you in prayer throughout all my living. I am weak in this; I am weak in praying always. Help me with this, gracious Savior. I may want for a lot of things. Please forgive me when I want more than you and I want things before I want you. For my life, even now as I am praying, I am thinking of what I still want to control. I still want what I want. Oh, my God, take this want from me and replace it with a want for only you. "Whom have I in heaven but thee? And besides thee, I desire nothing on earth. My flesh and my heart may fail, but God is the strength of my heart and my portion forever (Psalm 73:25–26). Help me, I pray, to truly let go of my attempts to control, for the more I try to control my life the less prayer will control my life. Help me, like our brother Paul, learn to be content in whatever circumstances I find myself in. Help me surrender my all to you—in prayer—so you can and will control all my life. In this there is prayerful peace deeper than the oceans and wider than the heavens (Philippians 4:6–7). Thank you for this truly wonderful, mysterious and intimate gift of prayer, Lord. Thank you for lifting me up and away from this troubled world to your glorious and high throne of grace and abundance (Psalm 69:29–30; Heb. 4:16)."

Day Twenty-four

the Gift of My Absolute Truth—
Your Freedom and Joy
(Part One of a Three-part Gift)

&

And you shall know the truth, and the truth shall make you free.

John 8:32

(This might be a little deeper than your typical Christmas stocking, so get that stocking off the mantel and give it a good shake to get out all the goodies that have fallen to the bottom.)

What is it you most look forward to when the Christmas season comes around? Could it be the parties, the gift exchange, the *Christmas tree adventure,* getting together with family and friends, or the songs and cherished traditions? Some might even say the shopping! Wow, can you believe that? Now that is a real Christmas season trooper. Or might it be the reflection and worship of the true meaning of Christmas—Jesus the Savior? Wow, what a concept! Now that is a true Christmas disciple!

What is it you are celebrating when you are celebrating Christmas? Are you celebrating the traditions you have perhaps grown up with—is it just something you do because it is something you have always done? Are you celebrating because it is part of our Christian heritage as a nation, or because it is what everybody else is doing? Are you celebrating the *joy* and festivities of giving and receiving gifts? (A good questions to ask yourself is, *does this time of Christmas incite in me a more self-ish or selfless attitude?*) Or perhaps for a lot of us, are you just celebrating—*trying* to get into the "joy" of the season because you are supposed to?

Do you know if what you are celebrating—Christmas—is based on a truth from God, or is it based on just man's idea of a religious or humanistic or fanciful need for comfort, purpose, and a sense of *oneness of mankind?* Do you really live out what you believe about Christmas? Why do you believe what you do? These are heavy questions to be sure, but they are questions we must have answers to if we are to experience the true wonder and mystery and joy of Christmas.

Truth: we need truth in this day when there is so much personal speculation, philosophic wisdom, scientific hypothesizing, and humanistic reasoning about truth and what life is about. This is why his gift of truth is so wonderful and so needed today. This is a day when not many people stand up for any kind of standard of absolute truth (this is politically incorrect), much less godly truth (this is definitely politically incorrect). It is a day when many people, like Pilate asked, "What is truth?" and then go about their lives without attempting to find the answer to their own question. If truth be told, this question produces an agonizing emptiness that only the truth and person of God can answer, which a lot of people just don't want to take the time or effort to find for themselves. They go about their lives unexamined, living on the superficial level of fleshly appeasement and pleasure. The depth of introspection and moral reason and conviction seems to be only skin deep, where the pleasure sensors lie in the flesh. Though truth can certainly bring about great security and peace, it can also bring about a lot of discomfort and pain as we dare to look deep within to see the error of our prideful ways.

A lot of mankind in this day and age believe *this or that* but do not know why they believe *this or that*. Without knowing why one believes what they do, produces a life that is indeed only skin deep, with little if any soul penetrating conviction. It is kind of like thinking we are celebrating Christmas with only the decorative window dressing of lights and decorations. All this is only a distraction in and to one's life, concerning the needed truth of Christmas. Qualities of selfless love, personal integrity, brotherly kindness, a pursuit of holiness, and a resilient and effectual faith are strangers, and in fact, cannot exist in this shallow environment and anemic atmosphere of our culture of tolerance and of our spiritually compromised soul. Conviction lasts only as long as there are personal rewards and pleasures and the exaltation of self. As soon as life gets uncomfortable today, we move on. We do not stick it out; we take the easy way and take off—physically, emotionally, and spiritually. There is little truth and conviction in our culture today and in the culture of our soul; thus, everything is relative and superficial. A true love, a godly love characterized by selflessness and sacrifice, cannot flourish or exist in such conditions.

Truth has been an invaluable commodity throughout the history of man. Satan confronted Eve with, "Indeed, has God (really) said?" Eve did not stay true to the word and truth of God. She bit into the doubt, the deception, and the lie from the fruit of the Devil's mouth. He created doubt in what God said, what God desires, who God is and who God made her to be. There have been lies and deceptions ever since. Pilate, a man in a strong and influential position, thinking that he was confronting Jesus (it was actually God confronting Pilate), asks Jesus, "What is truth?" Pilate did not know the truth. He did not know about the truth, and he did not have the truth in him, yet he was seemingly hungry for the truth. Whether Pilate was sincere about his question or not, at least he was asking the right person to get a right answer. It is a bit ironic that Pilate had the author of truth and the very personification of truth standing right before him but could not see the truth. He was blinded to the truth by the very real distractions (decorative window dressing) of his made-up *false truth* of his position, possession, power, and wisdom in his own mind and life (Proverbs 18:11–12; 16:25).

Science, which is presumably a discipline in search of answers, facts, and truths, is hardly that anymore today in our "anti-God" society. Many scientists today enter into their research and theorizing with the presupposition that there is no God; thus, they will interpret their data accordingly, even though the data may show them there has to be a creator, or at least some form of intelligent designer. There are many scientists that state that evolution is no longer a theory, but is a fact–it is scientific *truth!*

Atheists believe in and set their lives around their "truth" that there is no God—no Creator! Philosophers state that *there can be no absolute truth;* therefore, there can really be no truth that transcends man and his search for identity, meaning, and purpose. He is just an evolved animal trying to survive in a world with no standard of morality, ethics, law or government. The field of psychiatry and psychology work on the premise that man is the center attraction in life, and God, if he exists at all, is not the one true Almighty; nor is he the answer to man's life and problems, but in many cases, is the problem.

Truth is certainly a valuable commodity, especially around this Christmas season, as many see this time as a time of reflection of their own life, purpose, and mortality. Inspired by a little baby born in a manger and the holy life of Jesus as he walked this earth, we wonder, *what is Christmas all about, and how does this truth affect my life? Could such a fanciful and incredible story of God becoming a baby, born of a virgin, be true? What does this really mean to my life?*

We need truth now more than ever. If we could be discerning as we look around us, and within us, we might see that we live in a time and culture of relativism and tolerance for all of man's opinions and lifestyles. We live in a time when "fact" is manipulated into misinformation and used to deceive us. This is even true about Scripture as so many men and women will misuse the Word to fit their own philosophies and lifestyles (Gal. 1:6–7). We are susceptible to the media and information power mongers who have an insatiable clamor for control, power, and knowledge and information. Unfortunately a lot of the knowledge and information we acquire is not truth; nor is it based on truth, but is rather based on personal subjectivity, speculation, and self-glorifying presumption and desire. It is "misinformation" spun by the powers that be. (We won't even touch what politicians do with power. This is Christmastime, a time for joy and laughter!) Without a standard of absolute truth to live by (which is what truth really is—absolute, by definition), then that which is not truth will only lead us down a path of being trapped in personal doubt, confusion, insecurity, indecision, and even paralysis.

☙

"Father in heaven, now more than ever I so need your truth today. This Christmas season, I pray to let your Christmas truth shine, for there are many who do not know what the truth of Christmas and life is all about. There are many who want to do away with Christmas and Jesus and his truth. In the *evolving* "global community" with a root premise of tolerance and acceptance that seems so intolerant and antagonistic, if not violent against you and your Word, I pray you would secure us in the truth of your Word and in the truth of Christmas."

☙

"I confess, Lord, I do not appreciate this wonderful gift of your truth as I should. My life could really be made emotionally calmer, intellectually clearer, and faithfully steadier and stronger if I only rested upon your truth for my life. Help me do this, Lord. Help me do this today. It is your truth that is the beacon of light to bring me home to your heart as I travel though the dark and muddled storms of this life—storms within and storms from with out. It is your truth that is the foundation on which I can build my life when the world is doing its best to shake the foundation of your Word and truth (Psalm 11:1–3; 53:1–3; Matthew 7:24–27; John 17:17; 2 Timothy 3:16–17).

"You are a sure foundation, a refuge and stronghold, a very present help in trouble. I will not fear though the earth should change, the mountains slip into the heart of the sea, though its waters roar and foam, though its mountains quake at its swelling pride" (Psalm 46:1–3). "In spite of all these things, I will trust in your unmovable and unshakable and absolute truth of your word and your life in me" (Hebrews 13:8).

"Thank you, Lord, for your truth. May your truth shine ever so brightly this Christmas season and every day to illumine and do away with the darkness of all that which is not true, all the erroneous thinking arrogantly espoused by man that we have let imprison us. We need your standards of truth to live freely, joyfully, and abundantly as you will. We need your truth to keep us from going wayward. We need your truth as a leash of your love and life to keep us safe and bound to you. For from this truth—from your truth, comes love, grace, and freedom. And from this freedom in you comes pure joy which is, you."

৪৩

I am pleased to give you my gift of truth, my child. It is quite true that should you look to my truth your life would be at much more peace. As it is, you are shaken and your heart trembles because you are being bombarded with so many lies about yourself, about me, and the purpose and ways and meaning of life in this world "under the sun." This is the work of the devil, who is the "father of lies" and who has come to steal away and destroy the peace and purpose and joy of my spiritual abundance I desire for you (John 10:10; 8:34).

You are in a battle that is as real as any battlefield on earth (Ephesians 6:12; Romans 8:5–11). This battle-field is right in your home, in your school, it is where you work and live and play and go to worship. You do not even have to leave the comfort of your own bed, for the battlefront is in your mind—your think-ing—and it is about truth. Truth can easily get down-graded to subjective thought as man reinterprets truth and puts his own "spin" on truth to justify and fit his wayward lifestyle. This leads to irrational correspond-ing actions, attitudes, and emotions as you live day to day. Again, think about the truth Eve had; it was sure and true from my Word. She had no reason to doubt; she was emotionally and spiritually secure in my truth. Think about what information the devil was teasing/tempting her with, what thinking and emotions this may have elicited, and what she then did with such information in her emotional flurry, fleshly desire, and intellectual doubt. Things can get real ugly real fast when you hold to no standard of truth. The devil uses half-truths and misinformation—subtle lies that may seem logical if not enticing to lure you away from my truth. He wants to capture and imprison you, destroy your witness of me, steal away your joy, and then ulti-mately destroy you just like he did with Adam and Eve.

I hope you accept my gift of truth this Christmastime because with this gift there are marvelous freedoms freeing you from much error that keeps you bound and wrapped up in yourself rather than wrapped up in me (Galatians 5:1, 13). Where I am, there is freedom, because where I am, there is truth (2 Corinthians 3:17; John 14:6; 17:17).

Because you have my truth to guide your life, you

have standards of my holiness and gentleness, my goodness and love in walking you securely through this battle zone (Isaiah 41:10–13; Psalm 27:1–3; 44:6–7). You can rest upon my truths and know you have an unshakable foundation to your faith and your day-to-day, moment-to-moment living. Let my truth give you strength and confidence in a world demanding you to bow to its gods and views and principles of life. Merry Christmas, my child of truth. May you continue to grow in the knowledge and truth of Father almighty and be blessed in all you do (Ephesians 3:4–21; 2 Peter 1:1–4). Merry Christmas, my child. May my truth truly set you free to enjoy my full life for you (John 8:32).

ಜ

"Dear Jesus, you are the truth of my life. There is so much that comes from your truth, this I know. But little do I live in your truth. For some reason I choose to live in the version of my own truth—that which I can understand and that which I can manipulate and control to fit into and justify my own life. I am bound in erroneous thoughts this way, Lord, and this only leads to undisciplined actions and wayward emotions, which circle back around to feeding the mind with more erroneous thinking, emoting, and acting. My way of thinking and the accumulation of all my knowledge can be put in the smallest of boxes. Your way of thinking and your knowledge is limitless and cannot be bound. My way of thinking leads me to frustrations and questions that imprison me in myself. Your way of thinking is liberating, freeing me to experience all I can be in you and all you can be in me. As high as the heavens are above this earth so are your ways and thoughts so far above mine (Isaiah 55:8–9). Protect me from the deceit and schemes of the devil and my own flesh (1 Peter 5:7; Romans 8:5–8; 2 Corinthians 11:14–15). Oh how I need this protection of your truth, Lord, O how I need this protection. Strengthen me to trust no longer my own ways and wisdom, but to let go of my self-deceptive lies to truly trust in you and your truth. Thank you, gracious Lord. Help me walk in your truth today and forever more.

Day Twenty-five

the Gift of My Absolute Truth—Your Freedom and Joy (Part Two of a Three-part Gift)

❧

… and the truth shall make you free.

John 8:32

For you were called to freedom, brethren; only do not turn your freedom into an opportunity for the flesh …

Gal. 5:13

(This gift I believe is one of the greatest gifts we could ever receive and live in, I hope you agree. I am glad it falls on the twenty-fifth of December.)

The nineteenth-century Christmas carol states it best, "God rest ye merry gentlemen, let nothing you dismay, for Jesus Christ our Savior was born this Christmas day. *To save us all from Satan's power* when we were gone astray, Oh tidings of comfort and joy; comfort and joy. Oh tidings of comfort and joy." What awesome liberating truth there is in this short statement of truth: saved from Satan's power equals freedom, which equals comfort and joy!

Have you ever *gone astray?* Silly question, I know. Do you know what causes us to *go astray?* This is not so silly of a question. We go astray when we turn from the *protection of the truth* of the Lord for our lives to live in the false security (lies) of our own making (Proverbs 18:10–11; Psalm 49:13–20; 39:5–6; Luke 12:15; Rom. 1:18–23). It is when we walk in our own strength, following our own way for our own purposes. We are stepping out of the Lord's control of our lives where there is peace and contentment, and stepping into our own attempt at control where there is strife, contention, and jealous, envious, and insatiable want. When we do this, fear and discontentment enters in, and we begin a slow downward spiral toward struggle and hurt not only for ourselves, but also for those in our lives, not to mention grief for our gracious Lord. When we do this, we enter into the domain of Satan, where we allow his power to severely influence, dominate, and inhibit the godly wonderful and beauty of our hearts, minds, and lives. Solomon says it so simply: there is a way which seems right to a man (his own way), but its end is the way of death (Prov. 16:25). Sadly we do not know the end is a way of death–a death of joy and purpose and life in and for the Savior.

The truth that brings *comfort and joy* is Jesus Christ our Savior born on this Christmas day. A Savior for you and me, a Savior to save you and me and to set us free!

Christmas is about God's truth, and a blessing of God's truth is freedom. The "spirit of Christmas," if you will, is all about good news of great joy that a Savior has come to free us from our sin and from our self and from the lies of our flesh, the world and the Devil. The Savior has come to give us his truth as a beacon of light and life in guiding us out of the darkness of ignorance, presumption, self-righteousness and errors as we blindly grope for significance, wisdom, purpose and truth. We have built our own prideful *tower of Babel* that has served not to make our lives full and prosperous, but only to imprison us in the dungeon in the "tower of Self" - idolatry. The Savior has come to free us from the prison of a life of selfish want and idolatry. This prison only produces greed, envy, spiritual blindness, inner turmoil, loneliness, insecurity, despair, and fear, to name only a few things. He has come to liberate us from these things in his holiness, joy, and perfect and good love.

Fear not, let nothing disturb you, for Jesus our Savior, the sovereign ruler over all things, came in the flesh and was born on Christmas day. *Fear not* are the Spirit's words throughout the holy Scripture, perhaps more than any other exhortation. Though the world may lay in the hands of Satan's power for the time being (2 Corinthians 4:4; Matthew 4:8–9; Revelation 20), we can "fear not" because we are free from Satan's power (1 John 4:4; Romans 6:6–7), and in God's perfect love we are actually free from fear itself (1 John 4:18). "Fear not," Jesus says, "I have overcome the world (John 16:33) and the power of Satan" (Hebrews 2:14; 1 John 3:8). "Fear not," says Jesus, "I am in the midst of the storm with you and I will quiet the storms" (Matthew 8:23–26). "Fear not, let your heart not be troubled, though you feel lost and out of place in this world, I am preparing a place for you in the heavens, and I will return to receive you unto Myself that you will be with me forever" (John 14:1–3).

Imagine yourself in a jail or prison. In this place you have no rights, and each day is a severe emotional, spiritual, and physical struggle just to survive. There is great fear of the unknown and of not being in control. There is great fear of being hurt or killed, and there is great doubt with little hope and less if any freedom to say the least. What would be your greatest desire in a situation like this? I imagine your greatest desire would be your freedom. To make this a bit more personal, let's say you are in bondage; that is, you are imprisoned to an erroneous thought. Now do not think this any less of a prison. This mental, emotional, and spiritual prison we put ourselves in is just as real as a physical prison. You may not have physical bars to deal with, but you have a bondage that can be even more crippling. You know that you are in charge of opening these emotional prison gates at any time if you really want to, but you frustratingly cannot; actually, you will not. Thus, this prison is made even more despairing to your soul.

So, to lighten the analogy a bit (I do not like the thought of prison, especially at Christmastime or anytime for that matter), here is an untruth, a lie you tell yourself: Every day you wake up you just know that if you eat Christmas cookies, a treat you really like by the way, you will die (let Christmas cookies represent a fear or obsessive thought that is controlling you). You are absolutely convinced of this. This is truth to you. Therefore, you never eat Christmas cookies. You witness most everybody you know eating Christmas cookies and not dying. The truth is they are really enjoying them! Regardless of the objective evidence of the safety of eating Christmas cookies, you have this subjective and emotionally based fear that you will die if you eat Christmas cookies. You are captivated, no, let's say it more poignantly, you are severely imprisoned and crippled by this fear. You are controlled and held ransom by this fear. For the most part, your life is without true joy or freedom because of this fear, because of this untruth that you *feel* is truth.

This fear is like a wild animal. It does not like to be contained and certainly does not want to be done away with. This fear does not want to be restricted to eating just cookies. This fear, like the monster it is, wants to encompass every part about you—it wants to control your whole life. It wants to destroy your God-given image of the real you, your God-given confidence in him, your God-given freedom and passion to serve and live for him and others, your God-given hope to endure victoriously, your God-given relationships to enjoy and grow in, your God-given need and joy of worship of God, and your God-given desire to enjoy every part of life. It wants to destroy you!

What you need is freedom from this fear, right? And this freedom from fear, from error, from self-made prison and paranoia, freedom from self, is what Jesus gives you as his Christmas gift today (and every day)! He tells you that you do not need to fear eating Christmas cookies and that you will surely not die if you do. He tells you that if you live in this fear, this fear will envelope you and control you, it will be the idol you serve (Philippians 3:19; 2 Peter 2:19). "But", he says, "if you give me this fear, and let me give you my sovereign love and freedom, then your heart will smile, and your face will smile, and those around you will smile, and I will smile, and you will be filled with joy" (and all of God's people will say, 'Amen!'" 1 Peter 5:6–8). He tells you the opposite of what you (and the world) have been telling yourself. Why? Because he loves you and wants you to walk in freedom and spiritual abundance of joy with him. He tells you that you will be blessed because you are obeying his call to freedom rather than obeying your fear (Psalm 1:1–23; 40:4; 84:5; 91:1–4; Proverbs 2:1–12; 3:13–18; Galatians 5:1, 13). Are you ready to receive this gift? He is ready to share some cookies with you. Let's share some Christmas cookies and open this gift of freedom together.

ॐ

"My Lord and Savior, thank you for your gift of truth, which brings forth freedom. Thank you for setting me free from the power of sin and the devil. Thank you, Lord, for setting me free from fear and my obsessive thoughts about self. Forgive me, Lord, when I choose to not walk in this freedom but choose to walk in fear. I really do want to walk in this freedom of life you have blessed me with, but at times my emotions and my self-centered heart deceives me and binds me, and I am caught in this struggle with fear. I am blinded by this fear as I allow my fear to close my world into a small and shrinking black box where all I can see is darkness and have so very little air to breathe. I am suffocating!

"I need your light of truth, the truth of what Christmas is all about, the truth of your life and why you came. Lord, as you know, I am too easily swayed by the whims and at times the uncontrolled ravings of my emotions as I let my thoughts and fears of all that I cannot control, control me. Help me see your splendor and majesty and sovereignty over all there is, so I may experience the freedom of your Christmas gift and message."

My child, I know where you are, what you are feeling, and I hear your concerns, worries, and fears before you are even aware of them. I know your dreams and aspirations. I know your weaknesses and strengths. I know you better than you know yourself (Psalm 139:1–6). I would ask that you would trust me and let me love you, for it is only in my love for you, as you chose to walk by faith in this love, that your fears will be taken away (1 John 4:18). You must give them to me, though, I will not take them from you unless you ask. And you must do this in faith, not resting on your feelings. Your feelings can be tremendously crippling to the joy and freedom I wish for you. Do not trust your feelings for they will often mislead you, trust in my truth. From my truth I will bless you with my true emotions as you do this, emotions of joy and peace, which will lead you to contentment and security. Together we can destroy your fears, and we can do this right now!

You have a fear of losing control of your life. This cripples your life by not letting me be in control. You have a fear of what others say about you. This cripples your life by not listening to me and what I say about you. You fear failing, or not succeeding, or disappointing others. This cripples your life by not letting me live through you in my wisdom and strength and letting me be your judge and your purpose. You fear not being loved and you fear being rejected and left alone. This cripples your life by not letting me be the first love in your life and the first lover of your soul. You fear not living up to the world's standards. This cripples your life by compromising and neglecting the purpose and power I desire for you. You fear not living up to my standards. This cripples your life. Oh my child, you cannot live up to my standards by yourself, this is impossible. My standards are perfect and holy and absolute. As you surrender your life to me, then I will live through you in my holiness and righteousness, and together we will find freedom in your life you have never experience before.

It was for freedom that I set you free (Galatians 5:1, 13), so that you no longer have to be enslaved to the power of sin and Satan and self (Romans 6). You are free from the judgment and penalty of sin, death, and free from the entanglements of your weak and impulsive and emotional flesh. You are free from the opinions and ways of this world. You no longer have to be tied to the reasoning and wisdom of finite man in giving you a purpose and identity, in satisfying your need to feel loved and accepted and valued, in providing for you thoughts of emotional healing and well-being. In me you are healed. I am your Healer, so now go and live no more for yourself. Sin no more and walk in true freedom (Luke 5:24; 7:48–50; 8:48).

You are now free to not have to "keep up with the Joneses." You do not have to have the most or know the most or be the best looking or to have achieved more than anybody or everybody else. You are free to not live in fear of man, not live in comparison or competition with man, or not live in being a slave to man. You now have an option to be free in serving me. My yoke is easy and my load is light (Matthew 11:28).

You are free from the prison of your own perceived and made-up self-image. You are not who you see in a mirror, or what you feel within your soul, and you are not even what you think, especially when you think wrongly about yourself, which is what you do most of the time. You are who and what I have made you to be, my child, my friend, my servant, my representative, my love. You are freed from your self, the darkness of your flesh and heart (Jeremiah 17:9). You are free from the priorities and ways of this world. So, my child, walk in this freedom, walk in this newness of life and no longer in the prison of self (Romans 6:4; 11–12; 13:14).

Do you fully realize what this means? You are now free to be who I made you to be. Do not be tied to a mere distorted and perverted image you see of yourself in the reflection in the mirror of this world, but be free to rejoice and revel in the true image of who you are in me! You see, my wonderful Christmas child, if you live in fear in this world, you are not living by faith in me. I have made you not to live by fear, which is what your fleshly sight produces, but to live by faith, which produces freedom and joy. Fear robs you of taking steps of faith and being confident in me, which is the only way you will have confidence in yourself. Fear keeps you from being vulnerable and emotionally trusting and intimate with others which are so important for your life. It weakens and sickens your true self so that you do not grow in me, and thus, end up desperately and futilely hanging on to a dark shadow of your fallen nature of a deathlike life. I have set you free from all this. Come to me, take that step of faith, and believe in yourself no longer. Trust me and let your faith in me overwhelm your fear of the world and even yourself. Live freely in me (John 16:33).

Living by fear is a choice. So is living by freedom. So choose to live in me and receive this wonderful gift of freedom that is my life and my joy in you. May you be blessed this Christmas morning to have cookies with me. This gift is yours for the opening and appreciating. Let us enjoy your life and have fun together!

ॐ

"Lord, this gift of freedom is a most wonderful and ever-expanding gift. In contrast, it is my fear and desire to control that puts my life in an ever-shrinking black box of frustration, desperation, and despair. As I look around my life and see so many places where I feel trapped and caught in the ways of the world and flesh, I long to experience your Word to come to life and truly free me from my prideful and foolish chains that have kept me bound for so long (Psalm 119:18–20; 38–40; 81–82; 145–149). Thank you, Lord, for setting me free by your truth. Thank you, Lord, that I can fearlessly take steps of faith, even toward places I am not sure about because I know in you there is great freedom from any and all fears, worries, and concerns that would otherwise paralyze my life. Thank you, Savior, for such a gift as freedom in you."

Day Twenty-six

the Gift of My Absolute Truth— Your Freedom and Joy (And Love and a Bunch of Other Fruits of the Spirit, Part Three of a Three-part Gift)

&

These things I have spoken to you, that My joy may be in you, and that your joy may be made full.

John 15:11

But the fruit of the Spirit is love, joy …

Gal. 5:22

The stockings were hung by the chimney with care …"

O f the many Christmas traditions, of all the fun time around the tree and the table at Christmastime, there is one tradition that if we did without, the Christmas celebration would just not be the same. At least that is what my sister would think, even at an age of, shall we just say … well, she is out of grade school, not to mention high school, college, graduate school … and almost entering into the school of retirement (some traditions we just cannot grow out of).

For many, the favorite tradition might be the Christmas dinner. Others would certainly say it was the exchange of presents. Others might cherish singing on Christmas Eve, going to church service, sharing with neighbors, caroling, and the list can go on and on. But there is one little extra goody that I know this one in my family would never do without. That is the Christmas stocking, hung by the chimney with care in hopes that "goodies stuffed to overflowing would soon be there" (or something like that). Wonderfully decorated, generously stuffed, and overflowing with many goodies, the Christmas stocking is simply, preciously, childlike. Never mind that the stocking may be filled with some useless stuff and candy that no one should partake of alone; it is the childlike excitement of the many things packed into the Christmas stocking, then ever-so excitedly dumped out on the floor, that is fun.

Before we leave our thoughts about Christmas and these O so wonderful gifts from our gracious Lord of Christmas, we must look at his gifts of his Spirit, bundled together in his "Christmas stocking" of his character and love and life he so desires to share with us each day of the year. His Christmas stocking, if you will, is hung in our hearts with care, just waiting to be opened as he wills in our lives. There is an important condition to consider as we would enjoy these gifts, that is, he is the one who does the opening of these little wonders. And for him to do this, we must let him into our hearts, fully, uncompromised, and without condition. For this most precious Christmas gift to be enjoyed, we must surrender our all to him so then in return he can be his all in our lives through these gifts. They are his gifts to us to share with others, through us. That is his purpose and his will. That is what Christmas is all about—his life given and shared with us, so together with him we will share his love and life with others.

So, let's see just what these little packages of personal life and power that are stuffed in his Christmas stocking in our hearts are all about. We have previously looked at his truth that sets us free. And we have begun to understand that we are free in him to live fully, no longer bound to the lies and power of Satan, and no longer bound by a self-full fear that robs us of his joy. And now that we are free we can truly experience his joy, a joy that runs deeper in us than any poisonous root of fear or doubt could ever run. It all starts with his love, which is one of the greatest truths for our lives. As we allow his love to control our lives and as we love him in return, his fruit of love, joy, peace, patience, etc., will burst forth in abundance blessing others, honoring him and making our lives flourish as we could never have imagined.

&

"Dear heavenly Father, precious Jesus and wondrous Holy Spirit, thank you for this gift of Christmas celebration. I realize, Lord, that we impulsive human beings have certainly lost a right perspective about Christmas. In my self-centered heart living in this material world I have lost track and focus of the greatest gift of all—you in my life. This day and from now on, I come back home to your heart so you can work in and through my heart to be you to another (John 13:34; Ephesians 5:1–2).

"Your gifts of the Spirit are so contrary to how the materialistic and narcissistic world lives. To walk in love, to be patient, kind, good, to be peaceful and joyous, to be faithful, to live in self-control and to be gentle would mark us as being somewhat strange in this world (Psalm 119:19; 2Cor. 2:14). Lord, help me live this way. Help me be a little strange as the world would see me, in a strange and alien world (Philippians 3:20). Help me, Lord, surrender to you my all so you can be your all through me (Eph. 3:14–20). I pray to be your willing and humble servant in serving your Word of love and grace and truth and holiness to your creation. Use these gifts in my life to bless others. Use these gifts in my life to bless, honor and glorify you. There can no greater usage of these gifts than this—that you be blessed and honored and glorified.

"My gracious Father, may you grow in me the fruit of Your Spirit. May I be solely abiding in You and no longer in the world. Forgive me for abiding more in the world than in you. This has only produced weeds of discord in and around my life which has grieved you and dishonored you. Help me sever the roots of want and lust from the tainted soil of this world that you might be glorified in my life. Help me make this celebration of Christmas an everyday celebration of joy of your life and will in my life. Thank you for tending to me as your precious garden in which you desire to grow much fruit (John 15). May I be open to your cultivation of your will and purpose in me. May your will be done in this way, Lord, may you will be done in my life."

಄

My first gift to you is my love, my Christmas child. Without love, you have nothing and can do nothing (1 Corinthians 13). Without love you will only make a discordant noise in your life that people will not want to hear. As I love you, my child, love others (Ephesians 5:1–2). Let this fruit encompass everything you do and say. It is my perfect love that will cast out your fears (1 John 4:8) and carry you along when things seem a bit tough (Romans 8:35–39). I will produce this love in you and it is this love that will supply you with all you need to carry out my desire and purpose for you. It is in the truth of my love to you as you receive and rest in this love that you are free. And it is this freedom from the bondage of error and fear that my *joy* may overflow your life.

಄

Rejoice always I say, rejoice always (1 Thessalonians 5:16). Take my joy, the joy I had when I temporarily left my throne in heaven to put on the flesh for you, the joy I had to live my thirty-plus years for you, and the joy I went to the cross for you (Hebrews 12:2; James 1:2–4; John 15:13). Die to yourself and with a joyous heart and desire, live for others as I have lived and died for you. Your willingly joyful heart is good medicine (Proverbs 17:22) and just what one person may need as you allow me to live in and through you. This joy is a supernatural experience of joy and cannot be found or imitated by anything in this world. This joy comes from resting in my love and sovereignty knowing that nothing will ever separate you from me. This joy comes from knowing that I am in absolute control over absolutely everything that makes up this life. If love is the color and foundation of my gifts and life in you, joy is the loudspeaker singing songs in your heart of my life for others. As you let your heart and your day to day living sing of this joy, an overwhelming experience of *peace* will flood you and control you.

Wherever you go, I am with you and my peace will prevail (John 14:27; 16:33). The countenance about you will be of my peace (Psalm 34:5; 89:15). Through trial, persecution, and suffering, as you let go of the things and priorities in this world that you are trying to control, my peace will be the quiet voice of my love and faithfulness for you that will lift your spirit to the high place of the heavens (Psalm 18:19, 33; 31:8; 118:5). A quiet peace that I will bring alive in you will speak loudly in your endurance and surrender to my will. Others will see this peace and want what you have. Let me show them my peace through you. It is a peace that surpasses understanding (Philippians 4:6–7) and can only produce a peaceful heart in you. This peace gives you great strength to not fret or be bothered by this life (John 14:27; 16:33). This peace is a foundation for *patience* in living in this restless world that will try you and push you to an extreme.

My strength in patience I give to you. Patience and endurance takes strength that only I can give you (Psalm 37:1–7; 40:1–3; 46:10; 57:1–3; 62:1–2, 5–8). Rest not on your own strength when you are ministering and living for me. In your strength you will fail (John 15:5), but resting in me, I will never fail through you (Isaiah 40:28–31). Be patient and do not grow weary in doing good (Galatians 6:9). Though the world will test you, friends will turn away from you, even betray you, be patient with them. It is my will that none should perish, but that all should come to repentance (2 Peter 3:9). As I am so patient with those who turn away, like the father of the prodigal, be patient and look out to the horizon for many to return home. Rest in me, understand and know and experience my love, and let your heart overflow with life-changing and life-controlling joy. Let this joy bring forth great peace as you no longer have to strive in this world for what is in the world (Psalm 46:10; 1 John 2:15). As you rest in me and depend on me, do not fear what man can do to you (Psalm 56), but in my love be patient and at peace with all men as far as you are able (Romans 12:18).

Be kind in all you do. Show acts of kindness in my name (Philippians 2:1–8; John 10:30–37, 13:15). To do this, to allow me to show kindness though you, rest in me, and allow me to work through you. If you are to pray for your enemies, if you are to love those who do not love you, if you are to not return evil for evil (Romans 12:9–21), and do all this with kindness and goodness, then trust me to give you all you need (Philippians 4:19). Remember you can do nothing in your flesh, but by my Spirit you can do wonderful things (John 5:20). The world will hardly know what to do with such kindness (1 Peter 3:15–16). Your willing acts of kindness will definitely catch their attention, and in this you can show the world the goodness of my heart, and perhaps some may even realize the truth and be saved from the snare of the devil (2 Timothy 2:24–25).

Goodness comes from the heart, a genuine compassion and empathy for wanting what is best for others. As I am in you and as you allow me to live through you, you will reflect my goodness. Put another's interests before your own. Lay your life down for your neighbor first in your heart, then live selflessly giving your life for my purposes this way. The goodness that I will produce in you will take you out of thinking of yourself to sincerely thinking of others. It will take you out of a life of self. As you follow my ways and trust and obey, as you surrender to my will, my loving kindness and goodness will shine forth.

Of all the great and wonderful qualities of friendship, there is none more important than faithfulness. I will be faithful always. Though you will at times be faithless and at times walk your own path, I will always be faithfully there for you. A lot of relationships are about control and power. Mine are not. I want relationships to be about selfless love and faithfulness. In practicing these things, power and strength is yours as you rest upon me in your relationships. I could have deserted you on the cross and could desert you now, but I did not and will not do this because I can not deny myself (2 Timothy 2:13). Do so likewise for one another. Be faithful to me and let me give you the strength to be faithful to one another.

As you walk this earth, be as meek and gentle as a lamb. Walk humbly with me and walk humbly with your neighbor (Micah 6:8; Romans 12:12–21). In humility there is great strength and power. Though the world does not see it this way, it is my way of life (Mtt. 5:3–12). I came as a sacrificial lamb; I send you out as lambs amongst wolves. But take heart; be not afraid. Your humble and contrite heart I will use for my glory and your blessing (Psalm 51:17; 1 Peter 5:6). Be meek and humble with one another, love one another. This is how the world will know you are mine and I am yours (John 13:34–35).

In this life you will be tempted to scream, to seek revenge, to give in to the temptations, to be treated fairly. Don't worry about such things. As you surrender to me, like all these other gifts, I will give you the gift of self-control and discipline (2tim. 1:7). As you look to me and rest in me for all your needs, you will find peace and contentment and have inner strength to walk in self-control. You will be able to do this because your eyes will be set on me and my provision and truth and perspective for your life. You won't need to react to unfairness that is ungodly. The more you come to know me the more you will trust and rest in me, and the more you can walk with self-control and grace. You will not have to hold on to your "rights", seek your revenge, make "things" right, or judge this errant world in which you live. You won't need to look out for number one because I will do these things for you. Rest in me and trust in me, and you will find no greater strength to live a life of love and peace and joy—a life of self-control.

଼ଠ

"Dear almighty God, Eternal Father, dear Savior and Holy Spirit, thank you for this Christmas reality. Thank you for Christmas. Without this truth, we would have nothing. May I be a vessel for you to use, my Lord. May you use me to bless others with these gifts of the fruit of the Spirit–your life in me. Continue to do a wondrous work in my life for your glory. Thank you for using such a one as me.

I pray in the name of Jesus and all for your glory. Amen."

My son, if you will receive my saying and treasure my commandments within you, make your ear attentive to wisdom, incline your heart to understanding. For if you cry for discernment, lift your voice for understanding; if you seek her as silver, and search for her as for hidden treasures; then you will discern the fear of the Lord, and discover the knowledge of God … for wisdom will enter your heart … Take hold of instruction; do not let go. Guard her, for she is your life

Proverbs 2:1–5, 10; 4:13

Section Three

Enjoying Christmas Everyday!

Day Twenty-Seven

How Do You Do Christmas Every Day?

ॐ

Christmas—when the Eternal came to clothe himself with the temporal (Isaiah 7:14; John 1:14; Philippians 2:5); when the Infinite came to experience the finite (Hebrews 2:17–18; 4:14–16; 5:7–10); when the Sovereign came to surrender his will to the point of death; (Luke 22:42; Hebrews 5:8; Philippians 2:8); when the Creator of all things came to put on the flesh of his creation and to save his creation (Colossians 1:16; Luke 19:10; Matthew 18:11). Christmas is truly mind-boggling to the finite mind. Christmas, such a story, such a truth could never come from the mind of man, but only from the mind of God.

Christmas is not just a day. It is not just a season. Christmas is eternal, planned out in eternity past, purpose for eternity future and lived out every day! Christmas is not really about Christmas trees, gift exchanges, flying reindeer, turkey dinners, or even Christmas stockings hung over a hearth while chestnuts are roasting in the open fire. Though the word and season of *Christmas* originates with man, the truth and essence of Christmas is truly beyond our ability to fully understand. Christmas is about the indescribable glory and holiness of God shining down upon and in the darkness of the heart of man. No man can see the unveiled glory of God and live, but we can see Jesus—the Word—God, who became flesh who dwelt among us (John 1:1–3, 14). This is what Christmas is about; Jesus stepping down from his throne of glory (John 17:5) in bringing us the gift of his life; and in so doing, an understanding of who God is, at least as far as we are capable of understanding such glory and magnificence (John 17:6; 14:9).

Christmas brings this incomprehensible glory and reality to the realm of man. Christmas brings the infinite and what would seem to be an impersonal God so vast and beyond our comprehension to be in intimate relationship with you and with me. Christmas unlocks the gates and treasures of the eternal and infinite heavens and blesses this finite speck of dust called planet earth and the Creator's most precious creation, you, with the riches and richness of his presence in glory in his holiness and love.

As we close out our thirty-one-day devotional look at Christmas, let us spend the last few days looking at this truth of, *Immanuel,* God with us, and what it takes to live in the power of his presence. This babe in the manger, Jesus our Savior, came to give us a new year, a new day, and a new hope—a new life, only through his saving blood and the power of the resurrection. And, he came not just to give us these things in some mystical or aloof manner, as if we have to stumble and blindly grope through life hoping to find his meaning and our purpose and value; he came to live not just with us, but *in us* (Colossians 1:27; Ephesians 1). His life and his gifts are of supernatural origin with supernatural power producing supernatural effects. It only makes sense that we need some wisdom and insight from above in being able to use and be used by our Lord and his gifts.

The million-dollar question is, how? How do we live this Christ-focused, this Christ-centered, this CHRISTmas life everyday? How do we truly experience his life of peace, purpose, and power, his glory and joy in us?

This is the million-dollar question. How?

In the following four days, we will look at just four ways (out of many) to better follow our Lord. They include: ceasing from striving; knowing our God; the principle of putting off and putting on; and, remembering.

℘

"Dear Spirit of God, may you bless me with your counsel and teaching. May my ears be open to your words of truth and guidance for my life. Thank you, mighty God, that Christmas is so much more than we see on the outside. It is infinitely more. Lord, I can never fully understand this majesty and glory of what Christmas means. I pray to only have the little I do know and understand vitalize and color my heart with awe, wonder, and majesty of your presence each and every day. Thank you for touching my life with your truth and presence. Let me live for you, to be in awe of you, glorifying you in all I think, say, and do. Only you are worthy to be praised. May my heart praise you for ever and ever, amen.

Day Twenty-eight

Cease Striving ...

&

Come to Me all who are weary and heavy-laden, and I will give you rest.

Matt. 11:28

Cease striving and know that I am God; I will be exalted among the nations, I will be exalted in the earth.

Ps. 46:10

Do you have a favorite Christmas goodie: Christmas cookies, chocolate-covered toffee, fruitcake (really?), eggnog, chestnut pies, apple pie, or candy canes? What do you have to do with these goodies to know they are your favorite? You need to taste them, right? This principle of "tasting" is equally important in our spiritual life. We must, as the psalmist says, "Taste and see that the Lord is good" (Psalm 34:8). With our fast-approaching New Year just around the corner, we need to set up a nutritional plan for some good food, food for thought and food for action that leads to a changed life (John 6:27).

Let's partake of some tasty morsels of Christmas (Christ-like) truth as food for thought in how to live for Jesus in his presence and power. And let us not compromise here and say, "Live more fully" for Jesus, as if we are measuring how much of ourselves we are willing to commit, but with reckless abandonment to any measure of self, let us decide that we are going to live completely without restraint for Jesus. Any attempt to live "more fully" for Jesus as if to "fit" Jesus into our lives where and when we can, is the "lukewarm" compromise and attitude that the Lord will spew from his mouth (Revelation 3:16; Matthew 19:16–26; Luke 18:9–14). As he has given us his all, so too do we need to give him our all! This is imperative for a life of peace and purpose! To live with abandonment to self and to live completely for our Lord we simply must *cease striving* to find self and living for self. Remember this life you have to live is not yours. It is his for his use for his glory (Galatians 2:20; 1 Corinthians 6:19–20; Phil. 1:6; Eph. 2:10).

To understand what it is to *cease striving,* let us see a bit of what we need to "cease striving" from. Let's look at Christmastime as a microcosm of what takes place in our daily life and what we cannot do should we desire to live completely for him. Some of what happens in this *most wonderful time of the year* is not necessarily a wonderful or a pretty sight. If we could take an honest look at that which controls us from within and from with out, we can see we accentuate and exasperate the already patterned daily worship of the idols, *self* and *things.* We quicken our already hectic pace and packed schedules to include buying presents, buying more presents, and buying too many presents. As fuel is to a fire, in this season of materialistic intoxication to please self, we see "sale" signs and get swept up in the impulse of the moment and justify buying things we cannot afford and things that we or others do not really need. To make matters worse, at times we actually compete within our family and friends to buy the more expensive gift that we might praise ourselves (and receive praise) for such generosity.

We prioritize getting together with friends and family, attending parties and get-togethers at work, parties at school, neighborhoods, and church. Our schedule is such that wherever we are going, we had to be there five minutes ago. We are moving at just a couple of miles per hour shy of *warp ten!* During the most wonderful time of the year, it seems the personalities of our fellow co-workers, schoolmates, friends, and even family become a little more irritating as our nerves are being bombarded and frayed with "holiday" busyness, pressure, and stress. We want to impress, and we want to pretend we have it all together, and we want to not disappoint. We set up a Christmas tree, decorate the house, we get lost in all the tinsel and glitter this season demands. We lose ourselves in the very decorative and bright "window dressing" that the world sees (and expects to see!) as Christmas. It is all external and very little if any, internal, and spiritual.

And so it is with our spiritual life, especially at Christmastime. We tend to spruce up, can we say *holiday up* the external to show off some sort of spirituality while at the same time, we neglect the inner necessity of meditation and reflection on the Christmas truth—Jesus. So much external window dressing, so many decorations outside, yet on the inside though the lights may be on, no one is home for Christmas. We are compromised as our motives for living are on gratifying our self-centered need for the surface dressing of pleasure and vain acquisition and accomplishment. Rarely are we content with where we are and what we have. We want to be in a better place, a higher place; we want more things to add to our attempt of finding purpose and value. We want a greater spiritual experience and satisfaction through the externalities of life.

Yes, a lot of the holiday goings on can be fun, but a lot of it only adds stress to our otherwise busy schedules and our already off-target priorities in living. Though we perhaps think about others, as we should during this Christ-centered time of year, we still are very much wrapped up in ourselves. If and when we give to others less fortunate than ourselves, we often do it to ease our perhaps guilt-ridden conscience of not being benevolent and compassionate throughout the entire year. We give because we think we should, not because we truly and empathetically desire to.

We lose the joy of Christmas - the sharing of lives, and the purpose of giving our lives to one another because we are just too much in a self-created whirlwind of activity. We lose the Person of Christmas—Jesus, in lieu of the worship of Santa (commercialization/materialism) and the worship of self.

Living in his Spirit of Christmas is a difficult thing to do. It is made difficult because we let the culture that is so contrary to the ways and principles and standards of our Holy God influence our thinking so dramatically. It is so very difficult to live in his power because we want to live by our own power, intellect, reason, and abilities. Our culture tells us to strive to acquire, strive to promote ourselves, strive and prioritize to meet the standards of modern-day materialistic goals, strive to know more, to have more, to control more, to move faster encompassing broader circles, to make faster business deals, to make things faster and to make things cheaper (this includes relationships!), to be connected to the Internet faster, to grow (up) faster, etc., etc. All the while God is telling us to …

Cease striving …

Psalm 46:10

ॐ

"Cease striving," the Lord exhorts. "Be still, stop moving, quit your futile attempts at religion, do not look any longer for your purpose and identity in anything other than me", we might hear Jesus expand on this wonderful little exhortation. And he might continue, "Stop all this stuff and this running around and all this trying to show off your independence and strength of person. Cease and desists all this fleshly futility and vanity and striving after the wind. Don't you know that this will get you nowhere? Do you not know this will only wear you out? Do you not know you will end up with nothing? Stop your striving and know that I am God. I will be exalted among the nations, I will be exalted in the earth. I will be exalted in your life." (This knowing is the key to our peace and our practical connection to him, which we will look at tomorrow.)

Wow, talk about a counter-command that goes against the grain of our fast-paced, *me-istic* (it is all about me) get-all-you-can-while-you-can manmade Christmas mandate and culture. The Savior was born on Christmas Day to save us from our self-destructive Christmaslike schedule and Christmaslike agenda going nowhere fast. He came to save us from what our culture has made Christmas to be—basically a practice of self-worship!

So, what do we need to do to stop this pending "sleigh wreck"? The answer is simple. Simply, stop, be still, cease striving, or least slow down a whole bunch to smell the pine of your Christmas tree. Wow, can you imagine that, during Christmastime to stop and be still? Even on Christmas Day do we really stop and come to know and reflect on the Savior in a new way? I dare say we do not.

If you want to know how to get in touch with the Savior—the wonderful Holy Spirit of Christmas residing in you and truly enjoy the gifts in his life for you, then you must do this. You must stop striving. You must be still. Stop trying to live life by yourself as if you are the most important person in your life (this will make those around you very happy). Stop striving to be religious in proving to others and to God that you are special in this way (this will make God very happy). Cease striving to make your life work without God in your life, which is what we all do when we do not pray unceasingly, when we do not invite him into all our decisions, when we live like the world on the outside even though we may say we hold to the Lord's teachings on the inside (this will make you very happy). Jesus simply invites us to (cease striving and) "Come to me all who are weary and heavy-laden and I will give you rest. (Cease striving and) take my yoke upon you, and learn from me, for I am gentle and humble in heart;

(cease striving and) you shall find rest for your souls. For my yoke is easy, and my load is light." (Matthew 11:28–30).

We need to replace all our "hamster-like striving" and futile activity with something. We need to replace our striving for self, with *knowing* him and resting in him. The psalmist encourages us to meditate on his Word—on the living Word, every day, night and day (John 1:1–3, 14; Psalm 1:1–3; Psalm 19; Psalm 119).

Meditate—what images does that word conjure up in your mind? Sitting out in a grass field or an incensed filled room in the lotus position chanting "oouuhhmm"? This is not what meditating is. Do you meditate on his Word daily? Before you answer this too quickly, realize one cannot meditate on God's Word on the freeway, running on a treadmill, or while on a ten-minute coffee break. We can think about him and even quote some verses (which is a good thing to do), but to richly and deeply meditate at a level that will change your inner life must come from a devoted and consecrated stillness from the days activities of other things.

We need to pray and read and then pray some more. This does not mean this is all we do. We still need to function in life. But what it means is that we no longer trust ourselves for anything. We no longer assign ourselves the title and position of "god of our lives" and we let God be the God of our lives. We surrender our worries, our troubles, our guilt, our fears, our whole life's purpose and value over to him. We need to have him constantly in the thoughts of our heart, wherever we are, whatever we are doing. We live, but we live no longer for ourselves in the flesh; we choose to live each moment for him by faith. We cease striving for self, and we start striving—resting, in him.

෨

"Thank you, my great King, that your ways are not man's ways; neither are your thoughts man's thoughts. Thank you, Lord, that you are so far above man and the pettiness and smallness of man, we cannot even imagine. Yet in your greatness and humbleness you are so intimately and compassionately caring for us. Help us, Lord, cease our silly little striving after things and images that mean absolutely nothing to you. We so easily get wrapped up in these fleeting thoughts and desires that we lose sight of you. We get so wrapped up in the external offerings of the world that we unwrap ourselves of your life and purpose and provision. Thus, we substitute that which is the real thing—you—for that which is false—the world. We exchange true internal joy that can only come from you with the shallow and very fleeting external happiness of things of this world. Bring us back to your heart. Bring us back to the quietness of life you desire for us. Help us truly be still and know you better.

Forgive me, Lord, when I withhold part of me in my attempts in living for you. Forgive me when I do not let you be the true and only Lord of my life. I surrender my all to you now and thank you for your patience in and acceptance of my life. Lead me beside your still waters and abundant pastures of plenty. May you be pleased to do so. Amen I pray, in the name of Jesus, Creator and Savior of all.

Day Twenty-nine

...Know That I Am God

&

Cease striving and KNOW that I am God...

Ps. 46:10

...but the people who know their God will display strength and take action.

Dan. 11:32

What do you know about Christmas? Did you know that Christmas was declared a federal holiday in 1870? Did you know that it was the Dutch that brought the tradition of Santa Claus to the Americas? Did you that that it was St. Nicolas of Turkey that is the origin of our present-day Santa Claus? Did you know that Christmas card first became popular in England, or that Martin Luther was supposedly the first one to put candles on a pine tree in Germany to celebrate Christmas, and that Thomas Edison came up with the first string of electric light bulbs for the tree?

There are gobs and gobs (gobbles for all us trivial turkeys!) of trivia out there about Christmas that can make one feel an expert on the Holiday. I wonder if they know that Christmas, the name and date on the calendar and the very celebration, has its roots in pagan religion? We may know a lot of "stuff" about Christmas, but this does not necessarily mean that anyone is an "expert." The question of course is, *Do we now the true meaning of Christmas and the God of Christmas?* Without knowing the God of Christmas, all the other "stuff" we might know is just a distraction that literally gets in the way of knowing what is crucially important (John 5:39–40; Ecc. 12:12). Many want to feel the joy and excitement of the Christmas season, and in this priority, many miss knowing the true joy and true peace of the true and only God of Christmas.

Knowing God: can one really know God? Yes we can. This is one of the reasons why Jesus came, to reveal the Father to us that we might know him and know him better (2Pet. 1:2, 3:18). We might know a lot of "stuff" about God and about Christianity, and about what is written in the Bible, but if we do not know God and are increasing in our experiential knowledge of God, all other information is almost useless (1Cor. 13:2). How do we feel secure in this life if we do not know the sovereign God of all security? How do we feel love and value in this life if we do not know the God of love who created us in his image? How do we know the purpose to living and what is going to happen after we die if we do not know the eternal God who has purposed us and holds our eternal destiny in his loving and holy hands?

The New Year is upon us. Though this transition from the old year into the new year is just a date on the calendar, we can use this time to think about and make some changes to our lives (no, I do not mean New Year's resolutions like going to the gym more often or being nicer to your teachers, parents, kids, spouse, employees, or coworkers). Let's enter into this New Year with a new Christ-focus instead of our old self-focus. Let us forget all the fleshly life that has gone on before us and look toward new opportunities the Lord will provide for us. Let us look spiritually by faith, not physically by sight. Let us grow in the knowledge of God, and let this motivate us and control us in all that we do (2Cor. 5:14; 2Pet. 1:3–9, 3:18).

What wonderful and tremendous insight the Spirit conveys to us through the life of Paul. Paul had it all going for him. He was a success in the eyes of his peers and religious community. He was smart, had power and status, he walked confidently in his beliefs and had a life that in the world's eyes was quite fulfilling. He did not have to worry about where his next meal was coming from or whether or not he could afford some luxuries for his life. He seemed to have it all together.

Then one day, everything changed for him. He met the Lord in a very up-close and personal way. The Lord blinded him for a time so he could restore his proper vision and perspective of what is vitally important—knowing Christ! The Lord stripped away the old Paul in order to make a new Paul, each new day (2 Corinthians 4:16). His whole life changed. He now saw everything from a different perspective and vision—no longer from his old eyes of flesh which Jesus touched (when that happens, nothing is the same!), but from the Lord's vision and perspective, by faith. From being a persecutor of the faith, he became a promoter of the Faith. From being an independent free thinker and slave of no one, he became a dependent slave of the Master, disciplining his mind to knowing Christ Jesus. He went from being self-righteous to being humble and finding a true Christ-righteousness as his only identity (2 Corinthians 5:17, 21).

In all the power and prestige and self-importance he had, after meeting Christ and entering into his new life, he considered everything he had as meaningless.

> But whatever things were gain to me, those things I have counted as loss for the sake of Christ. More than that, I count all things to be loss in view of the surpassing value of *knowing Christ Jesus* my Lord, for whom I have suffered the loss of all things, and count them but rubbish in order that I may gain Christ, and may be found in him, not having a righteousness of my own derived from the Law, but that

which is through faith in Christ, the righteousness which comes from God on the basis of faith…

Philippians 3:7–9

Paul's focus of life was turned from himself to the Lord. He was to no longer strive to know about himself and his religion, but was focused on knowing God and his kingdom. Paul was pushing forward, striving toward that upward call (Phil. 3:12–14). The Lord was his perfect portion now (Phil. 4:19; Psalm 16:5, 11), and there was nothing of his past that he needed in his life to feel complete. He used to think his religion was what made him righteous, and he strove to become more righteous in his religious work. After meeting Jesus he understood that righteousness does not come from the law (religion) or anything he could do, but from God alone, and this by faith.

There is nothing more important in life than knowing the Savior. There is nothing more captivating, challenging and revitalizing than this pursuit in the knowledge of God. Our minds will expand. Our hearts will be refreshed. Our lives will be focused in a way we could never have thought possible. In growing in the knowledge of his sovereignty and love, our fears and insecurities will fade away to nothing. In growing in the knowledge of his holiness and justice, we see and are more deeply grieved with our foolish ways and sin. In growing in the knowledge of his goodness and mercy, we will be inspired and strengthened to live likewise. In growing in the knowledge of his faithfulness, we will find rest from worry and doubt that stymies our faithful walk. As we grow in his truth and power, we will find victory over our temptations of the flesh and this world and the schemes of the Devil. As we grow in his wisdom, we will find insight and discernment in the foolish and deceptive and self-seeking world of want and pleasure (Col. 2:8). Growing in the knowledge of him is the greatest exercise and experience of life, and is his will for us.

May we all grow in the grace and knowledge of our Lord

and Savior Jesus Christ. To Him be the glory, both now and into eternity (2 Pet. 3:18)

ᏸ

"My Lord and my God, I am so easily satisfied with simply gaining knowledge about how to run my own life, my way. In fact I have to admit that this is my priority, in the flesh. My Father, I no longer want to live this way. I no longer want to be satisfied with knowing what I need to do for my self-focused life. I want to know you more and more. Teach me your ways. Teach me your truth. Teach me who you are. This Christmas season, this New Year, I pray to make my life's priorities on just this, knowing you. For when I do this, everything in my life will come into focus. In knowing you I will see what is important to you and that which is insignificant to you, thus, to me as well. Everything in my fleshly life that I think is important will pale and will lose its control over me when I grow in true and experiential knowledge of you. Thank you, my God, for your patience and desire to teach and lead me in the knowledge of you. Thank you."

ᏸ

> Not that I have already obtained it, or have already become perfect, but I press on in order that I may lay hold of that for which I was laid hold of by Christ Jesus. Brethren, I do not regard myself as having laid hold of it yet; but one thing I do; forgetting what lies behind, and reaching forward to what lies ahead, I press on toward the goal for the prize of the upward call of God in Christ Jesus.
>
> Philippians 3:12–16

We have been talking about necessity of growing in the knowledge of God in order to live in the power of Christ. Paul died to himself and took up his cross and followed Jesus. Paul knew what salvation was about. He believed himself to be crucified with Christ and that his life was no longer his own but the Lord's who bought him with his blood. He knew this life was now a life of faith, trustfully laying down any fleshly impulses and ambition he might have, to putting on a focus on the will and promise of his Lord. To live in the life and power of the Lord, like Paul, we must deny our self, die to our self, and let Jesus live through us (Mark 8:34–38). Paul became a disciple of Jesus instead of being a disciple of his own religion. He became a disciple of the present moment, if you will, no longer living on his laurels and reputation built up in the past or what he aspired to be in the future. He was a disciple of learning life from the Savior each new day instead of a disciple of the past, holding on to the security of what he thought he had made himself out to be. He counted all that he was before Christ and all that was outside of Christ—the non-vital priorities of life—as rubbish, as nothing!

He lived his life from this point on (after meeting Jesus face to face) in the constant mode of forgetting what lay behind and growing in the knowledge of God. His past, like yours and mine, would stealthily creep up behind him, seeking to grab him in its talons of guilt, past hurt, and past successes, luring him to be dependent on his prideful self. This is exactly what happens to us today! The remedy for Paul and us? He was daily forgetting; that is, he was choosing not to dwell on his memories and laurels, and putting his focus on the call of the Savior and the knowledge of the Savior for each new day.

Paul's life was no longer a life of religious duty, presuming that was a life of faith. He was now living a life of true faith by completely abandoning satisfaction of earthly need and resting totally on the provision and promises of Jesus (2Cor. 3:5, 4:7, 12:9). Paul pressed on. He strained forward. He disciplined himself to choose the life of faith and knowledge in Jesus. He made a deliberate and diligent effort to move from where he was to where the Lord was leading. Before Christ, Paul had a plan as to where his agenda would lead him. After Christ, he did not know where he would end up, but he knew that his purpose in life—Jesus, would be there all the way (Hebrews 12:2, 13:5; Phil. 1:6).

The Lord calls us to walk by faith and not by sight (2 Corinthians 5:7; Hebrews 11:6). He calls us to walk by faith and not by fear (or feelings or selfish ambition or intellect or even at times, common sense reasoning). He calls us to walk by faith in him and no longer to walk by faith in what we can see or understand in our own abilities. To walk in faith is to rise above and not be controlled by our feelings. Living by feelings will derail us quicker than we can say, "feelings will derail us." But if we could simply remember the faithfulness and love of God; if we could put off our striving to live a life on our own and forget what our life was about yesterday, good or bad, then we can find great freedom and strength to live each day fully as the Lord intends, by faith!

There is great joy, hope and truth in the Christmas message, in which we can look forward to the New Year and a new life. We can do this because God's joy and hope in our hearts are immovable, unshakable, and are eternal. They are based on truth and not feelings. They are based on the character of God and his forever faithful Word of truth providing for us all we need as we focus on growing in the knowledge of his life and his kingdom first (Matt. 6:32-).

&

"Thank you, Lord, for Christmas and the truth of your life. There can be no greater life than this, than to grow in the knowledge of you and to live for you. Thank you for all you have done throughout the year and throughout our whole life. Thank you, Lord, for calling us to be yours today and for leading us into wherever you would have us go tomorrow. May I cherish and treasure and use always your life gifts of Christmas. Help me use these gifts in the knowledge of your promises and character as I live for the lives of others. In doing this, you are honored and glorified. Thank you, my Savior, for choosing me and using me to accomplish your purpose and will here on earth. May each day I live be a Christmas day as I prayerfully give back to you this life you have given to me. Thank you, my Lord, for such a privilege and such a life. Thank you and amen.

Day Thirty

Put off/Deny and Put on/Practice

&

But put on the Lord Jesus Christ, and make no provision for the flesh in regard to its lusts.

Rom. 13:14

So, now that your Christmas presents are open, what do you do now? And what do you do with these *life gifts*—this life of Jesus in you?

The answers are the same, and it is quite simple. You wear your new clothes or you use your new toys (even at the age of fifty-five). You make a deliberate decision to put them on or use them. It is the same with the *gifts of life* of Jesus in your heart. You make a deliberate decision to wear them and use them. You make a decision to put them into practice. You practice the presence of God this way. You do this best by the way by giving thanks and by sharing them with others. You deny your old self and way of doing things and you begin to walk in the new ways of life with which he has blessed you (Colossians 3; Ephesians 4; 2 Corinthians 5:17; Romans 6:4–13; 13:14).

In laying a deeper foundation of this "putting off and putting on" principle, here are a few exhortation for us to follow: "Therefore consider ('reckon,' i.e., to know this to be true and live by this truth) the members of your earthly body as dead to immorality, impurity ... in them you also once walked when you were living in them. But now you also, *put them all aside* (put them off) ... since you laid aside the old self with its evil practices, and have *put on the new self* who is being renewed to a true knowledge ... *put on* a heart of compassion ... *put on* love which is perfect bond of unity ... "(Colossians 3).

"This I say therefore, and affirm together with the Lord, that you *walk no longer* ... in the futility of (your) mind ... that in reference to your former manner of life, *you lay aside* (put off) the old self which is being corrupted ... and that you be renewed in the spirit of your mind and *put on the new self,* which in the likeness of God has been created in righteousness and holiness of the truth ... " (Ephesians 4:17–32).

Listen to this battle going on in these words of the Spirit concerning the Spirit and the flesh:

> "For those who are according to the flesh set their minds on the things of the flesh, but those who are according to the Spirit, the things of the Spirit. For the mind set on the flesh is death, but the mind set on the Spirit is life and peace, because the mind set on the flesh is hostile toward God; for it does not subject itself to the law of God, for it is not even able to do so; and those who are in the flesh cannot please God" (Romans 8:5–8).

For the Lord to use his gifts and life through us we must put off our mind and heart of flesh and put on the mind and heart of the Spirit. Putting off the old, putting on the new, that is the principle to follow. This principle of "putting off" and "putting on" may not be as easy as we would like. Our flesh will rise to do great battle within us as we strive to put off the selfish appetite for pleasures of the flesh and put on the ways of our Lord

(Rom. 7:5, 15–25; 8:7). Let us not be deterred by this reality but to listen to the truth of the Spirit as he writes to us that we are new creatures, reborn in his Spirit, that all things have become new (2 Corinthians 5:17; John 3:3, 7). Let us therefore live in this newness of life and no longer in the oldness of the sinful flesh (Romans 6:4–11).

God does not want us to be confused about his life and blessings for us. He wants us to live in joy and freedom of his love and calling in our life (John 10:10; 14:27; 15:11). Does that surprise you? He came to destroy the works of the devil, to give us the very real opportunity to not live in the power of sin. If he says this, then we can do this. This may seem like a radical thought to us, but it should not be. He would not tell us what to do if it were not possible for us to do it. The difficulty lies in how much of our lives are really self-centered instead of God-centered. God does not want us to agonizingly struggle through life as we so often do. We agonizingly struggle because we are self-centered, not God-centered. We think for some reason that living this Christian life is all about trying to guess what God wants from us—about living a "religious" life. This will only tie us in knots, and it is not what Christianity is about. Christianity is not primarily about "doing," it is about "being"! Let us change this perspective to realize that God wants us to learn more of what he wants *for us* not *from us.* Let's put off this old way of thinking and put on his new way of thinking.

So, what we need to do is start today and choose right now to *put off* striving for our life and living for our self as we have done for so long. And in replace *put on* striving for him and start living for him. As the Apostle Paul implies, forget what is behind but look forward, strain forward to the upward call of Christ Jesus, not the lower call of the flesh. This must be a complete abandonment of your old life, which by the way has been crucified with Christ (Gal. 2:20), and a complete acceptance of his life in you and your life in him. You need to choose to surrender your life and all those decisions you make through the day over to him and strive to know him better and "return to your rest," as the psalmist writes. You need to strive to rest in him. I know that may sound a bit of a paradox, "strive to rest," but this is the way of our amazing and all-wise God (Matthew 11:28; Matthew 6:33; Psalm 46:10; Colossians 3:2; Isaiah 55). "The Lord preserves the simple; I was brought low and he saved me. Return to your rest, O my soul, for the Lord has dealt bountifully with you" (Psalm 116:6–7).

℘

This *putting off* and *putting on* is a process you do one step, one decision at a time. And it is something you must do daily. It is certainly not uncommon to *put off* a behavior or attitude today, only to foolishly *put it back on* tomorrow. This practice is a continual work while you live in the flesh. Realize you cannot do this by yourself; you need the Lord to do it with you.

Let us say you live in a world where the ultimate purpose in all of life is to play tennis—to be the best tennis player you can be. This is what mankind is all about. But right now you are a pretty good golfer and think highly of yourself. You have had success and have built a reputation and a name for yourself in your own (little) golfing world. You have become a good golfer because you have committed yourself to practice long and hard for this purpose. Because of this, you have neglected and even buried your innate inner calling to be a tennis player. You are not too bothered by squelching this "inner calling" or this "mildly disquieted void within you" because of your successes playing golf. You have busied yourself in your own world, living off your own efforts and priorities of succeeding in golf. Golf is your appetite, and for now you think your life is being nourished by golf.

Soon you realize that even though you are good at golf, in many ways your life is not as it should be. There is something missing, something that does not quite click and make your life come together in harmony with itself. Even though you are out in the beauty of nature, and life on the golf course seems serene and peaceful, there really isn't an inner peace that quiets your soul with a sense of fulfillment and contentment. Though you fight this inner turmoil you have a very clear sense that there is something that must come from outside of you to bring you purpose, value and contentment within.

Well, one day you are internally convicted that you must be true to your innate calling and pursue playing tennis. Tennis is now going to be what your life is all about.

If you want to be the best tennis player you can be, how would you best do this? Simple, you would take up tennis lessons, right? Right. This does not necessarily mean you would drop golf completely, but you would sacrifice (*put off*) some golf time for the much needed tennis time. As you begin your new adventure into tennis, you would not expected to be able to hit (tennis balls) with the best players on your first day out would you? No, of course not. Though in your vanity and pride you might think you can or that you belong with those who know the most or can do the most. After all, that was the way it was in your life as a golfer. The truth is you would need to learn tennis one step at a time, with beginners. This takes a humble nature which will be new to you. You would have to learn and practice the fundamentals over and over again until they were second nature to you.

In your learning and growing into becoming the best tennis player you can be, you would see times of little to no improvement, and at other times huge improvements with many plateaus scattered throughout. Along this new path there will be times that are tiresome and frustrating. You will be tempted to just give up and jump back on that pathway of playing golf because it is easier; there are less conflicts and obstacles, and most of your good friends are there. But as you grow in this new venture of tennis your mental, emotional and physical priorities and outlook begins to change. You are learning a new kind of patience and self-control you did not know you had. You are feeling better inside and you are meeting new friends that help support your challenges you face.

This journey is a slow process and sometimes painful, but with patience and sacrifice (of your old game of golf), you find yourself steadily walking, then jogging, then running on your new road of purpose to playing tennis to the best of your ability. You are steadily putting off your golfing priorities and way of life that was destructive to your tennis calling and life, and you are putting on your new life of tennis. It started as one little step (of humility perhaps), then two somewhat larger steps, then soon, playing tennis became second nature to you—you are finally at home, where you were designed and purposed to be.

These same principles apply to your learning and growing in the Lord. You must make deliberate choices to discipline yourself in sacrificing what is keeping you away from pursuing spiritual growth—putting off your old self, and in place of these distracting habits, form new habits of spiritual growth and training (Romans 13:14; 12:1–2; Colossians 3:1–3; Psalm 1:1–3; 2 Timothy 3:16). In changing your priorities, you will move away from yourself and move closer to God. Cease striving to fulfill self, put off your old ways of life, and take his yoke upon you (put on) and find rest, purpose, peace, and identity for your new life.

ဆ

"My Lord and my God, may you guide my life toward you and away from myself. Help me, Lord, to stop worrying about my life and my agenda worked up by my emotional self-centered priorities. Lord, I want to live fully for you and no longer for myself. Help me slow down. Yes, Lord, help me stop the direction I have been going and turn back to you. Forgive me for just 'lip-service' and little to no 'heart-service.' Forgive me for talking a surrendered life, but not living a surrendered life. Lord, help me to prayerfully stop at your throne in your presence and rest for your bidding in my life. Help me put off my old self of flesh and put on, daily, moment-to-moment, my new life—you. Be exalted in my life, dear Jesus, be exalted in my life. Amen and amen.

Day Thirty-one

Remember

&

I shall remember the deeds of the Lord; surely I will remember Thy wonders of old.

Ps. 77:11

What is your fondest Christmas memory? My mind is instantly flooded with many detailed pictures of the past. I remember watching the joy of my daughter as we anticipate and celebrate the Christmas season: Christmas morning, Christmas tree hunting, making cookies and hot chocolate, laughing over a story told about someone dear. I think back to when I was growing up and remember certain presents, both exciting and disappointing (yes, I was a bit greedy and misdirected then, believe it or not). I remember Christmas Eve night at my grandparents' and taking a walk late at night, looking up into the starry sky trying to find Santa's sleigh (I could have sworn I did see a flickering reddish light scraping the darkness). And I will never forget one particular singing performance of "O Holy Night" at a Christmas Eve service. It was as if an angel was singing; the voice and music were so clear and majestic.

Our reflection will also bring us face to face with some not so fond memories, memories that distress our soul and spirit. There are many tearful and deep-hurting memories and emotions of lost ones, missed ones, and broken relationships and broken hopes and dreams. I remember one Christmas Eve when the whole family arrived at my parents' for our traditional Christmas Eve festivities. We had to take my mother to the emergency room. She has been sick for a while, but we did not know how sick. She had almost died that night. And there is loneliness and even despair that grip hearts as many are alone at Christmastime, left alone in memories hoping things were different, then and now.

Memories are a part of us. They are part of what makes us think what we think, do what we do and feel what we feel. We cannot avoid memories that can hold such influence over our present lives, but we can take control of these memories so as to not have such power over us. What can we do? We can *put off* these memories by replacing them with (*putting on)* remembrances of our gracious God.

Christmas is about the glory of our God shining down upon man in the form of the person of Jesus Christ. Christmas is about a new hope, a new perspective, a new life, today and with each new day. Christmas is certainly about God getting in touch with you and me; it is also about us getting in touch with the Savior by remembering and meditating on what he has done for us. David writes in one of his psalms, "Why are you in despair, oh my soul, and why have you become disturbed within me … Oh my God, my soul is in despair within me; therefore I remember Thee from the land of the Jordan" (Psalm 42:5–6). Do you hear his answer for his troubled soul? *Therefore I remember Thee …* Therefore, I will remember what the Lord has done!

We may have little to no hope in life. We may think God is a million miles away if he is anywhere. We may have little to no desire to even look up to the heavens in hope that someone is there and cares. Listen to these wonderful words inspired by the Spirit to comfort our hearts:

Then I said, "*It is my grief,* that the right hand of the Most High has changed." I shall *remember* the deeds of the Lord; Surely I will *remember* Thy wonders of old. I will *meditate* on all Thy work, I will MUSE on Thy deeds. Thy way, O God is holy; what god is great like our God? Thou art the God who workest wonders; Thou hast made known Thy strength among the peoples. Thou has by Thy power redeemed Thy people ...

Psalm 77:10–15

Though "Christmas," had not yet taken place when Israel was wandering in the desert for those many years, God's presence, power, and purpose were real to them. We can learn a little from this time in history in helping us understand a secret to making our lives work. Though God's mode of operation was different with Israel as it is now with us his Church, he remains the same. He loved (and loves) his people Israel and in this love he disciplined his people. He loves his Church, you and me, and in this love he disciplines his Church.

God was leading his nation Israel into the "promised land," a land flowing with milk and honey—a very productive and promising land we can say. But, Israel lost patience. They lost sight of their God. They lost their reverence for God. They lost their desire, their hunger and thirst for God. They wanted what they wanted and they wanted it when they wanted it. Listen to these few words from Psalm 106:

Our fathers in Egypt did not understand Thy wonders; They *did not remember* Thine abundant kindness, but rebelled by the sea ... nevertheless he saved them for the sake of his name; ... so he saved them from the hand of the one who hated them and redeemed them from the hand of the enemy ... they *quickly forgot* his works; they *did not wait* for his counsel, but craved intensely in the wilderness, and tempted God in the desert. So he gave them their request ... they made a calf in

Horeb, and worshipped a molten image, thus they exchanged their glory for the image of an ox that eats grass. They *forgot* God their Savior, who had done great things in Egypt … they despised … they did not believe in … but grumbled … and served idols, which became a snare to them … nevertheless he looked upon their distress when he heard their cry and *he remembered* his covenant for their sake, and relented according to the greatness of his lovingkindness …

Wow, don't you just love that last part, he heard their cry and *he remembered!* As often as we forget to look to him and remember his greatness of love, he *remembers* his love and knows our frame and is still patient with us.

୫

"Dearest Lord, may you be forever praised for your faithfulness and never-ending love. Your grace is truly amazing and your love unfathomable. Forgive me, Lord, for my neglectful lifestyle of not remembering you and all that you have done and continue to do in my life. As I look back, even in the dark times, I see your faithful and patient love. Forgive me for not acknowledging back to you, for thanking you for all that you have done. My life is truly blessed because of you. Help me see my life from your perspective, the true perspective that can only bring my life into proper focus. Thank you, Lord, that though in my daily living I choose not to remember you, you always choose to remember me, and look upon me, and hope for me, and extend your hand of grace to lift me from where I am to where you are (Ps. 18:33). Thank you for such love and desire. Thank you for such a life."

୫

As we remember him from an actual experience in our lives or from his living Word of truth, bringing to our minds his reality is a sure way to make his life real in our day-to-day routines. Let us remember and give praise to him for who he is and for all that he has done in our own lives and throughout the history of man.

Remember he is perfect and holy, and everything he does is perfect (Psalm 89:14; 99:5, 9)

Remember he is faithful, and all he does is out of his mercy and goodness (Psalm 145:9).

Remember he loves us with a love unconditional we will never fully understand and that nothing can separate us from his love (Romans 5:8; 8:35–39; Ephesians 3:19).

Remember that while we were yet sinners he died for us and that He paid the penalty of our sins–death. It is because of him we have life with the Father (Rom. 5:8; John 3:16; 1Cor. 15:3–4)

Remember he has a purpose and plan for us that we could hardly imagine (Ephesians 2:10; Jeremiah 29:11).

Remember he has been enduringly patient with us (as we might describe it) waiting for us to come to him, waiting for us to learn what we need to learn, and waiting simply to receive his blessing of love and life (Luke 15:11; 2Pet. 3:9; Joel 2:12–13).

Remember that God is absolutely all powerful and is the Creator of all things and that we are enclosed in his righteous right hand (Psalm 103:19; 139).

Remember that he lives in our lives in the person of the Holy Spirit (1 Corinthians 3:16).

Remember that we have his power to live our lives above temptation from within and from with out (1 Corinthians 10:13; Acts 1:8).

Remember just as he was with his disciples in the storm, so he is here with us (Matthew 28:20; Deuteronomy 31:6; Psalm 16:8).

Remember, just as he took care of five thousand-plus people for lunch, he will provide for us, with leftovers! (Psalm 16:5; 73:26; 145:14–16).

Remember he is with us in the morning when we rise, when we enjoy his provision throughout the day and is with us as we go to sleep. In this truth we can say: "In peace I will both lie down and sleep, for Thou alone, O Lord, dost make me to dwell in safety" (Psalm 4:8; 121).

Remember that he "sustains all who fall, and raises up all who are bowed down ... Thou dost give them their food in due time. Thou dost open Thy hand, dost satisfy the desire of every living thing. The Lord is righteous in all his ways, and kind in all his deeds. The Lord is near to all who call upon him, to all who call upon him in truth (Psalm 145:14).

As we close our heavenly Christmas devotions, let us always remember and never forget to see the faithful love of Jesus throughout all our life. If you want his life and his gifts to be a Christmas gift for one another every day of the year, cease your selfish ways of gain, set your mind to know him more and more, put off your old ways of living and put on his new ways, and meditate/remember the love and grace of the Almighty in your life. Remember his sacrifice for you. Remember the truth of his Word for you. Remember that every day is *a heavenly Christmas* day because Jesus is in it, in you, and you are in him.

ಜ

"Thank you, my Shepherd and Caretaker of my heart and life. Thank you for remembering your goodness and love and dealing with me accordingly. Thank you for remembering my sins no longer and blessing me with your abundant life. May I remember you always. I need to remember you far more than I do. Help me do this, Lord, help me do this. Help me treasure your Word in my heart so when the storms hit, I can quickly remember your grace and sovereignty. Help me remember that when I am hungry and without, you fed thousands. Help me remember when I am blinded by own lust of the flesh, you sacrificially and selflessly died for me and desire me to live likewise for you and for another. Help me remember that when I am surrounded by antagonistic views about you and feel some attack and persecution, you have been there yourself. To suffer with you is to live with you in peace and purpose. Yes, Lord, it is your sovereignty and your goodness and holiness I must remember to find rest for my life as I see your right hand of power guiding and protecting me. Lord, it is your love I need to remember that will cast away all fear of man and this worldly life. Help me remember this, Lord. I pray remembering your great love and desire for me. Thank you for Christmas, your Christmas gift of your life in me. May I give my life to you so you can live through me to be a Christmas gift to those you bring into my life. I pray in the name of Jesus, a name I will never forget and choose to always remember, amen."

> I will lift up my eyes to the mountains; from whence shall my help come? My help comes from the Lord, who made heaven and earth. He will not allow your foot to slip; he who keeps you will not slumber. Behold, he who keeps Israel will neither slumber nor sleep. The Lord is your keeper; The Lord is your shade on your right hand. The sun will not smite you by day, nor the moon by night. The Lord will protect you from all evil; he will keep your soul. The Lord will guard your going out and your coming in from this time forth and forever.
>
> Psalm 121

Merry Christmas all. Can't wait to see you on the other side, in heaven! Until then, make every day *A Heavenly Christmas Day: Enjoying the Presence of Jesus* to the fullest. May he be praised and exalted with all our body, soul and spirit, with all our strength. Amen? Amen and amen!

Epilogue

Parting thoughts–Christmas:
An offer we cannot refuse

&

T he thief comes only to steal, and kill, and destroy; I have come that they may have life, and might have it abundantly (John 10:10), says our Lord. The Author of Christmas intends for us to enjoy his life everyday. He *richly supplies us with all things to enjoy* (1Tim. 6:17). *In his presence there is fullness of joy; in his right hand there are pleasures forever* (Ps. 16:11). *Seek first my kingdom and my righteousness,* he says, *and all these things shall be added to you* (Matt. 6:33).

The Father God offers us Jesus his Son as the way to abundant spiritual life. Jesus came so that if we should choose to believe in him he would give us eternal life. *For God so loves you that he gave his son that whoever (you) believes in him should not perish but have eternal life* (John 3:16).

This is an offer we really cannot refuse.

If you do not know the Lord, that is, if you have not confessed your faith in him as Savior and Lord of your life, then you can do so right now. He is waiting to hear from you to give you his gift of eternal life and take from you your sinful nature. Going to church is not the answer, serving in church, being a good person, giving your time, money and energy to the less fortunate is not the answer in achieving peace with God. The answer for your eternal life with him is in a personal relationship with him, and this begins with this simple prayer. Pray this prayer from your heart and become a gift to him that he will always treasure:

> *Dear Father God, thank you for your love and patience for me. Thank you for Jesus, born on Christmas day. Forgive me for living for myself all these years instead of living for you. Thank you for sending your son to die on the cross for my sins, and to be resurrected that I might have eternal life. I give my life to you and joyfully receive the Christmas gift of Jesus in my heart. Lead me from this day forward in growing in the love and knowledge of you. In Jesus name I pray.*

If you have just prayed this prayer, welcome to the family of God and the wonder of celebrating a true heavenly Christmas everyday. Seek out a Bible teaching Church and enjoy growing in the fellowship in the Body of Christ.

If you have known the Lord for some time but have been walking your own path, take this time to recommit yourself to him. He is waiting for you as well to return to him that he might bless you with a renewed and vital purpose and life in him.

Once again, Merry Christmas all, and may each day be a Christmas celebration of his life in us as we share his life with others.